Herod and Mariamne

UNC | COLLEGE OF ARTS AND SCIENCES
Germanic and Slavic Languages and Literatures

From 1949 to 2004, UNC Press and the UNC Department of Germanic & Slavic Languages and Literatures published the UNC Studies in the Germanic Languages and Literatures series. Monographs, anthologies, and critical editions in the series covered an array of topics including medieval and modern literature, theater, linguistics, philology, onomastics, and the history of ideas. Through the generous support of the National Endowment for the Humanities and the Andrew W. Mellon Foundation, books in the series have been reissued in new paperback and open access digital editions. For a complete list of books visit www.uncpress.org.

Herod and Mariamne
A Tragedy in Five Acts by Friedrich Hebbel

TRANSLATED BY PAUL H. CURTS

UNC Studies in the Germanic Languages and Literatures
Number 3

Copyright © 1950

This work is licensed under a Creative Commons CC BY-NC-ND license. To view a copy of the license, visit http://creativecommons.org/licenses.

Suggested citation: Hebbel, Friedrich. *Herod and Mariamne: A Tragedy in Five Acts by Friedrich Hebbel.* Translated by Paul H. Curts. Chapel Hill: University of North Carolina Press, 1950. DOI: https://doi.org/10.5149/9781469657349_Hebbel

Library of Congress Cataloging-in-Publication Data
Names: Curts, Paul H.
Title: Herod and Mariamne : A tragedy in five acts by Friedrich Hebbel / by Paul H. Curts.
Other titles: University of North Carolina Studies in the Germanic Languages and Literatures ; no. 3.
Description: Chapel Hill : University of North Carolina Press, [1950] Series: University of North Carolina Studies in the Germanic Languages and Literatures.
Identifiers: LCCN 51000895 | ISBN 978-1-4696-5733-2 (pbk) | ISBN 978-1-4696-5734-9 (ebook)
Subjects: Herod I, King of Judea, 73 B.C.-4 B.C. — Drama. | Mariamne, consort of Herod I, King of Judea, approximately 57 B.C.-approximately 29 B.C. — Drama.
Classification: LCC PD25 .N6 NO. 3

INTRODUCTORY NOTE

The better works of foreign literature should be available to the reading public in English translation. The more nearly they are reproduced in the form and spirit of the original, the more such works enrich our own great store. It is with this in mind that I have translated Hebbel's masterpiece *Herod and Mariamne*, probably the greatest German drama of the nineteenth century.

Christian Friedrich Hebbel was born in the village of Wesselburen in Ditmarsch, Holstein, on March 18, 1813. He died in Vienna on December 13, 1863. The gloomy bleakness of northern Germany, the poverty of his home, the strict and sometimes violent discipline of his father had a permanent effect on his character. His was a serious, sensitive, imaginative nature, strong-willed even to the point of obstinacy.

Convinced early in life that he was to make his mark as a writer and a poet, he left his narrow provincial home and devoted himself to the achievement of his literary aims with an unswerving fixity of purpose—in spite of hunger, hardship, and disappointment. He endowed the characters of his dramas with the same fixity of purpose which he himself possessed, with a rigid, unswerving, relentless adherence to a point of view.

Hebbel was persuaded that the most tragic situations of life arise, not necessarily from any moral guilt, but rather from conflict between the individual will and its environment, and that this conflict is most significant when a vital change is taking place in the existing state of the world. His most important dramas are located at such critical times in history. In its early stages the conflict between the old established order and the representative of the new order is tragic for the new, but suggests hope for a brighter future. Such a conflict is the core around which most of Hebbel's tragedies are built. The individual undergoes a process of inner change and must inevitably suffer in a conflict with the whole, but the new cause is advanced, although it be but slightly. The Hegelian philosophy: thesis, antithesis, synthesis, is presented here in dramatic form.

The tragic story of Herod and Mariamne has appealed to many dramatists. For all of them the only historical source is Flavius Josephus in *The Jewish War* (75 A.D.) and *The Antiquities of the Jews* (93 A.D.). Hebbel is the first of these dramatists for whom the historical events are merely the background and for whom the real drama lies in the inner psychological development of the characters.

Herod was the King of Palestine from 37 B.C. to 4 A.D. The action takes place in the period just prior to the beginnings of Christianity. Though really an enlightened monarch for his day and even a reformer, Hebbel's Herod knows only the traditional methods of procedure, he still represents the old tyrannical order and represents it more completely as the play develops. From our point of view the change in him is retrogressive. Although Mariamne can be just as ruthless as Herod toward those beneath her, there is in her the first suggestion of the new order. Conscious of her own worth as an individual, she expects trust and confidence from Herod. When she does not receive them, life loses all value for her, and she deliberately brings on her own death at the hands of Herod. Less rigid and unyielding characters might have reached a compromise. With characters such as Hebbel depicts, tragedy is unavoidable. Herod is not only in love with Mariamne, he is an Idumean and a king, as Mariamne is a Maccabean and the daughter of Alexandra. Try as he will, Herod cannot forget the king for love of Mariamne, nor can she forget the Maccabean for love of him (*lines 1005 ff.*). Tradition and heredity are too strong for them. The necessity for tragedy lies within the characters themselves, not outside of them in a superhuman power. This is the modern fate tragedy.

A forerunner of Ibsen and naturalism, Hebbel was too early for his contemporaries. The performance of *Herod and Mariamne* in Vienna in 1849 and that in Berlin in 1874 could not but fail miserably, for neither the public nor even the directors and the actors understood either Herod or Mariamne and the nature of their tragic inner struggle. With the turn of the twentieth century appreciation began to dawn and since then this drama has appeared with fair regularity on the important German stages, reaching a high of 158 performances in one season. *Herod and Mariamne* will never enjoy wide popularity with the masses. To appreciate Hebbel the audience must think as well as feel, and that is not the mood in which most people attend the theater.

Hebbel wrote his drama in unrhymed iambic pentameter. The form is that of the classic German drama. The language, however, is straightforward, realistic, contemporaneous. It is the common language of his day, not colloquial, but simple and dignified. To produce as nearly as possible the same effect in translation, I have used a dignified, straightforward, modern English, avoiding exalted diction on the one hand and obvious colloquialisms on the other. I have tried to express Hebbel's ideas as he might have expressed them, had English been his medium. Translation in this spirit is a difficult task in prose, doubly so when it must be metrical and at the same time faithfully render the meaning of the original. Even with the difficulties it is surprising how literal the translation can be.

The translator desires to express his appreciation to Professors T. Moody Campbell, John C. Blankenagel, Homer E. Woodbridge, Arthur R. Schultz, Richard Jente and Frederic E. Coenen for their constructive criticism and many helpful suggestions, and to the Research Committee of Wesleyan University for the financial grant, which helped make publication possible.

PAUL H. CURTS.

Middletown, Connecticut
1950

HEROD AND MARIAMNE

CHARACTERS

KING HEROD
MARIAMNE, *his wife*
ALEXANDRA, *her mother*
SALOME, *sister of the king*
SOEMUS, *Governor of Galilee*
JOSEPH, *husband of Salome, Viceroy in absence of the King*
SAMEAS, *a Pharisee*
TITUS, *a Roman captain*
JOAB, *a messenger*
JUDAS, *a Judean captain*
ARTAXERXES, *a servant*
MOSES
JEHU } *servants, as well as other servants*
SILO, *a citizen*
ZERUBBABEL and
PHILO, *his son* } *Galileans*
A ROMAN MESSENGER
AARON, *and five other judges*
THREE KINGS OF THE ORIENT, *later called Saints by the Christian Church*

Place: *Jerusalem*   Time: *about the birth of Christ*

ACT I

Castle Zion. Large audience room. Joab. Sameas. Zerubbabel and his son. Titus. Judas, and many others. Herod enters.

SCENE 1

JOAB *(advances toward the King).*
  I have returned!
HEROD.   Save your report till later!
  The most important business first!
JOAB *(stepping back, aside).*   Important!
  I thought the most important was to learn
  Whether or not our head still sits secure!
HEROD *(summons Judas).*
  Tell me about the fire!   5
JUDAS.   About the fire?
  So you already know the news I bring?
HEROD. That it broke out at midnight, yes. I was
  The first who noticed it and called the watch.
  If I am not mistaken, I woke you!
JUDAS. The fire is out. *(aside)* So what they say is true,   10
  That in disguise he prowls the streets
  While others sleep! We must be on our guard
  Lest careless words might sometime reach his ear.
HEROD. When everything stood wrapped in flame I saw
  A woman through the window of the house   15
  Who seemed benumbed. Was this young woman saved?
JUDAS. She did not want to be!
HEROD.   Not want to?
JUDAS.   No!
  She fought against them when they tried to take
  Her out by force, she struck at them with hands
  And feet, she clung with desperation to the bed   20
  On which she sat, and cried that she had been
  About to kill herself with her own hands
  And now a kindly fate brought death to her.
HEROD. She must have been demented!
JUDAS.   Possibly
  Her mind had been upset by pain and grief!   25
  Her husband had just died a while before,
  His body lay still warm upon the bed.
HEROD *(aside).* That I will surely tell to Mariamne
  And watch her while I tell her! *(aloud)* Probably
  This woman had no child! But if she had,   30
  I will take care of it! She shall herself
  Be buried richly and with royal splendor,
  She was, it may well be, the queen of women!

SAMEAS *(steps forward).* Be buried! That is not permissible!
   At least not here, not in Jerusalem!   35
   For it is written in—
HEROD.   Do I not know you?
SAMEAS. You had occasion once to know me, yes:
   I served the Sanhedrin as tongue that time
   When it sat mute before you.
HEROD.   Sameas,
   I hope you know me too! You hated Herod   40
   When he was young. You would have liked so much
   To make his head a present to the hangman.
   The man and king has now forgotten that,
   For you still have your own head on your shoulders.
SAMEAS. If for the reason that you let me keep it   45
   I must not use it now, then take it from me;
   That would be worse by far than losing it.
HEROD. Why did you come? Till now I never saw you
   Within these walls.
SAMEAS.   But that is just the reason
   You see me now. Perhaps you thought I stood   50
   In awe of you. I have no fear of you,
   Not even now when many men have learned
   To fear, who did not use to be afraid,
   Before Aristobulus met his death.
   And since the opportunity has come   55
   To prove to you that I am thankful, I take
   Advantage of it and give solemn warning
   Against an act which God the Lord condemns.
   Accursed are this woman's bones, for she
   Resisted rescue as a Gentile might,   60
   And that is quite as if she killed herself,
   And since—
HEROD.   Some other time! *(to Zerubbabel)* From Galilee!
   Zerubbabel, who was—I bid you welcome!
   The blame is yours, I did not see you sooner!
ZERUBBABEL. It is an honor, King, that you still know me!   65
                (points to his mouth)
   Of course these two great tusks of teeth I have,
   That make me like the cousin to a boar—
HEROD. I would forget my own face sooner far
   Than that of one who served me faithfully!
   When we were hunting robbers to their lair   70
   You tracked them best. What do you bring me now?
ZERUBBABEL *(beckons his son).*
   In fact not much! Just Philo here, my son!
   You have a need for soldiers, I do not,
   And this boy is a Roman, whom, it happened,
   A Hebrew woman brought into the world.   75

HEROD. What comes to me from Galilee is good!
  You may expect a summons soon!
            (Zerubbabel and his ston step back)
TITUS *(steps forward)*.   A fraud
  Which I discovered forces me—
HEROD.   Disclose it!
TITUS. The dumb speak!
HEROD.   Please be clear!
TITUS.   Your man-at-arms
  Who stood on watch before your bedroom door   80
  Last night with one of my centurions—
HEROD *(aside)*. Whom Alexandra recommended to me,
  My mother-in-law—I see!
TITUS.   He is not dumb,
  As everyone has always thought he was;
  He spoke aloud last night in sleep, he cursed!   85
HEROD. In sleep?
TITUS.   He fell asleep while standing watch,
  And my centurion did not awake him;
  He did not think he was responsible,
  Because he is not in the cohort with him,
  But yet he kept close watch, so as to catch him   90
  If he should fall. For it was early still,
  You were asleep, he did not want to rouse you.
  Then suddenly, as he is watching him,
  The dumb man starts to mumble, speaks your name,
  And calls down fearful curses on your head.   95
HEROD. Can the centurion have been mistaken?
TITUS. He would have had to be asleep himself;
  And that would be an omen worse by far
  For the eternal city than the lightning
  That struck the Capitoline wolf not long   100
  Ago.
HEROD. I thank you! Now—*(he dismisses all but Joab)*
              Yes, so things stand!
  Rank treason in my house, and in the crowd
  Of Pharisees defiance, bolder still
  Because I can not punish them at all
  Unless I make the fools appear as martyrs;   105
  A little love among the Galileans,
  No, mere attachment of a selfish sort,
  Because I am the bogey with the sword
  Who from the distance scares their rabble so;
  And—this man Joab surely brings bad news,   110
  He was too anxious to announce it to me.
  For even he, although he is my servant,
  Likes doing what will vex me, if he knows
  That I must act as if I did not notice!

    (to Joab) What news have you from Alexandria?   115
JOAB. I spoke with Antony.
HEROD.   A strange beginning!
    You spoke with Antony? I am accustomed
    To have the messengers I send received;
    You are the first who finds it necessary
    Thus to assure me that he was successful.   120
JOAB. They made it hard for me. They put me off,
    Time after time!
HEROD *(aside)*.   He stands then with Octavius
    On better terms than I had thought! *(aloud)* That proves
    To me, you failed to choose the proper hour.
JOAB. I chose each one among the twenty-four   125
    Of which the day consists; no matter how
    They urged, I did not leave the spot, not even
    When Roman soldiers offered me a meal,
    And then, since I refused it, jeered at me:
    He eats no food save what the cat has tasted   130
    And what the dog has torn to shreds! At last
    I was successful—
HEROD.   For a wiser man
    It would have been at once—
JOAB.   And was received.
    It was already night and first I thought
    He had me summoned merely to continue   135
    The sport the soldiers had in jeering at me,
    For when I came inside I found a group
    Of drinkers there, reclining at their ease.
    But he himself poured out a glass for me
    And said to me: Drink this to my good health!   140
    And when I courteously declined to drink it,
    He said: If I set out to kill this man
    I only need to bring him to my table
    For eight full days and on it place before him
    The tribute earth and sea have rendered me,   145
    He would not eat but only sit and starve
    And dying swear that he had had his fill.
HEROD. Yes, yes, they know us well. That must be changed.
    What Moses ordered only to prevent
    Their worshipping the Golden Calf again—   150
    If he was not a fool—this people still
    Observes as if it were an end itself,
    And so is like the sick man who, when healed,
    Continues still to take the remedy
    As if he thought that medicine were food.   155
    That must—Go on!
JOAB.   However, I was soon
    Convinced that I was wrong, for while he drank

He carried out all business of the state,
He named the magistrates, and made arrangements
To sacrifice to Zeus, heard auguries,   160
And interviewed the messengers who came,
Not me alone. It was quite strange to see.
A slave stood there behind him, ears alert,
A stylus and a tablet in his hand,
Ridiculously serious, recording   165
What he had said in his half drunken state.
Next morning then, still feeling the effects,
He reads the tablet through, or so I heard,
And holds to all it says so faithfully
That he—they say he swore this recently—   170
Would choke himself to death with his own hands
If in his cups at night he gave away
The world o'er which he ruled, and had thereby
Renounced his rights to any place within it.
Whether he staggers then, as well as when   175
He goes to bed at night, I do not know;
That seems to me to be of no import.
HEROD. You win, Octavius! The only question:
   If now or later. Well?
JOAB.   When finally
   My turn had come and I had given him   180
   The letter which I had for him from you,
   Instead of opening and reading it,
   He tossed it to his clerk quite scornfully.
   He had his servant bring a portrait; this
   He bade me look at carefully and tell him   185
   Whether I found the likeness good or not.
HEROD. It was the portrait . . . ?
JOAB.   Of Aristobulus,
   The young high priest, who drowned so suddenly.
   The picture had been sent to him long since
   By Alexandra, by your mother-in-law,   190
   Who keeps in touch with him, and yet he gazed
   With greedy eyes as if 'twere new to him.
   I stood confused and silent there. He said,
   When he saw this: Perhaps the lamps are burning
   Too dimly here! and reached then for your letter,   195
   Set it ablaze and let it burn out slowly
   Before the picture like a blank white sheet.
HEROD. Bold! Even bold for him! But—he was drunk!
JOAB. I cried: What are you doing there? You have
   Not even read it yet! And he replied: 200
   I want to talk with Herod, that's the meaning!
   A charge of murder has been brought against him!
   And now he had me tell how this high priest

    Had come to die. And when I said to him
    A fainting spell had seized him in his bath,   205
    He interrupted: Seized! Yes, yes, the word
    Is chosen well; the fainting spell had hands!
    And so I learned—forgive me if I say it!—
    That they did not believe in Rome the youth
    Had drowned, but rather they were quite convinced 210
    That your own officers, at your command,
    Had strangled him while bathing in the river.
HEROD. Thanks, Alexandra, thanks!
JOAB.   He motioned me
    To go and so I went. But then he called
    Me back and said: As yet you have not answered   215
    The question which I put to you at first,
    So I repeat it. Is the picture like
    The dead man? When perforce I nodded yes:
    Is Mariamne like her brother? Does she
    Look like the youth who died so shamefully?   220
    Is she so beautiful all women hate her?
HEROD. And you?
JOAB.   First hear the comments of the others,
    Who left their seats and now were standing with me
    Around the picture. Laughing they exchanged
    Suggestive looks with Antony and said: 225
    Say yes! if ever he befriended you,
    Then you will see at least that he's avenged!
    I said however that I did not know,
    For I had never seen the Queen except
    When she was veiled, and that is really true!   230
HEROD *(aside).* Ah, Mariamne! But—I laugh at that;
    For I shall know how to protect myself
    From that, somehow, however it may come!
    (to Joab) What message did he give to you for me?
JOAB. Why none! If I had had a message for you   235
    I would not need to tell you all of this.
    But now I thought I must!
HEROD.   It's well! You shall
    Return at once to Alexandria
    With me and must not leave the royal palace.
JOAB. I shall not even talk to anyone.   240
HEROD. That I believe! For no one likes to die
    Upon the cross while figs are ripening!
    The dumb man shall be slain and should he ask
    The reason, say to him: Since you can ask!
    (to himself) And now I know through whom that wily serpent 245
    So often learned what I—A wicked woman!
    (to Joab) Take care of that! I want to see his head,
    I plan to send it to my mother-in-law!

ACT I, SCENES 2 AND 3

    (aside) She needs a sign of warning as it seems.
JOAB. At once!   250
HEROD.   One other thing! The Galilean
    Shall take his place, Zerubbabel's son Philo,
    I want to speak with him before we leave. *(exit Joab)*

SCENE 2

HEROD *(alone)*. Now comes the test! Once more! I almost said,
    But I can see no end. I'm like the man
    They tell of, whom the lion seized in front,   255
    The tiger from behind, and whom the vultures
    With beaks and talons threatened from above,
    While he stood on a nest of vipers! Good!
    I shall defend myself as best I can
    Against each enemy with his own weapons,   260
    Let that from now on be my rule and law!
    How long it lasts, that shall not worry me
    If I but hold my ground until the end
    And lose no thing that I have called my own,
    Then let the end come now, or when it will!   265

SCENE 3

SERVANT *(enters)*. The Queen! *(Mariamne follows him)*
HEROD *(goes to meet her)*. You steal a march on me, I was
    About to—
MARIAMNE.   Not to come yourself to get
    The thanks I owe you for your wondrous pearls?
    I have refused to see you twice, to try
    Again to see if I had changed my mind,   270
    That would have been too much for any man
    And certainly too much for you, a king.
    O no, I know my duty and since you
    Have heaped rich gifts upon me every day
    Since my gay brother's sudden death, as if   275
    You're wooing me anew, so now at last
    I come to show you my appreciation.
HEROD. I see!
MARIAMNE.   Of course I do not know just what
    Your purpose is. You send the diver down
    For me into the sea's dark depths and when   280
    No diver can be found who will disturb
    Leviathan's repose for money wage,
    You open up your jails and give the robber
    His head again, which he had forfeited,
    That he may serve you fishing pearls for me.   285
HEROD. And does that seem absurd to you? Why once

    I had them take a murderer from the cross,
    When there was need to save a child from flames
    That threatened it, and said to him: If you
    Can bring it safely to its mother, I   290
    Agree the debt you owe to death is paid.
    He plunged at once into the flames—
MARIAMNE.   And did he
    Come out again?
HEROD.   It was too late. I would
    Have kept my word and would have sent him off
    To Rome to fight, where they have need of tigers.   295
    It's best to make full use of everything,
    I think, why not of lives thus forfeit?
    For cases do arise where one can use them.
MARIAMNE *(aside)*. Oh, would he did not have the bloody hands!
    Best say no more! Whatever he has done   300
    Seems good when once he comes to speak of it.
    How frightful it would be, if he compelled me
    To find my brother's murder necessary,
    Yes, unavoidable and justified!
HEROD. So silent?   305
MARIAMNE.   Shall I speak? Of pearls perhaps!
    Till now it was alone of pearls we spoke,
    Of pearls which are so pure and clean and white
    That even in bloody hands they never lose
    Their lucid splendor! You are giving me
    Great heaps of them.   310
HEROD.   It troubles you?
MARIAMNE.   Not me!
    You surely can not wish to pay a debt
    With them, and it would seem to me I have
    A perfect right as wife and queen to pearls
    And jewels. It is quite right for me to speak
    Of precious stones as Cleopatra did: 315
    They are my servants and I pardon them
    That they cannot outshine the stars for me,
    In spite of that they do surpass the flowers!
    You have a sister, though, Salome—
HEROD.   She—
MARIAMNE. Well, if you aim to have her murder me,   320
    Then keep right on, despoil the sea for me,
    If not, then give the diver respite! I stand
    Already deep enough in debt to her!
    You seem to doubt? I lay a year ago
    Quite sick and close to death, she kissed me then.   325
    It was the first and only time. I thought
    At once: The kiss is your reward, because
    You are about to die! And so it was;

>   But she was disappointed, I recovered,
>   And now I have her kiss for nothing; that   330
>   She never has forgotten. So I fear
>   That she might think of that, if I should go
>   To see her with the pearls around my neck
>   By which you showed me last how much you love me!
> HEROD *(aside)*. The only thing that still is lacking is   335
>   That my left hand should turn against my right.
> MARIAMNE. I would at least disdain the drink of welcome;
>   If she should offer me instead of wine
>   A drink of water in a crystal glass,
>   I still would leave the water quite untouched: 340
>   Of course that would not mean a thing! No! That
>   Would even be quite natural, for water
>   Seems to me no longer what it was:
>   A gentle element that waters flowers,
>   Refreshes me and all the world; it sends   345
>   A shudder through me, fills me now with horror,
>   Since my own brother died so suddenly;
>   I always think, within the drop dwells life,
>   But in the wave there dwells a bitter death;
>   For you it must be very different!   350
> HEROD.   Why?
> MARIAMNE. Because you have been slandered by a river
>   Which dares unload its own inhuman and
>   Malicious deed on you; but never fear,
>   For I dispute it!
> HEROD.   Really?
> MARIAMNE.   I can do it!
>   To love the sister and to kill the brother,   355
>   The two can not be reconciled.
> HEROD.   Perhaps!
>   If such a brother is himself intent
>   On killing, and if one can only save
>   Himself by matching him, yes acting first!
>   We're speaking here of possibilities!   360
>   And further! If he, unsuspecting, lets
>   Himself become a weapon in the hands
>   Of foes, a weapon which must strike and kill,
>   If not destroyed before it has been swung.
>   We're speaking here of possibilities!   365
>   And if it threatens not a single head—
>   No, if it is the head of all the people
>   And one as necessary to this people
>   As ever any head to any body.
>   We're speaking here of possibilities!   370
>   I think in all these cases that the sister,
>   As wife because of love she owes her husband,

       As daughter of her people out of sacred
       Duty, as queen because of both of these,
       Must say: I dare not censure what has happened.   375
                (*he takes Mariamne's hand*)
       Although a Ruth might well not understand me—
       How would she learn it plucking ears of grain—
       A Maccabee will surely comprehend!
       You could not kiss me there in Jericho
       But surely in Jerusalem you can!   380
       (*he kisses her*) And if this kiss should rue you nonetheless,
       Then listen, and you will be reconciled:
       I took the kiss as my farewell to you
       And it may be, this parting is forever!
MARIAMNE.   Forever?   385
HEROD.   Yes! For Antony has summoned
   Me. Whether I return, I do not know!
MARIAMNE.   You do not know?
HEROD.   Because I do not know
   How harshly my—your mother has accused me.
MARIAMNE (*starts to speak*).
HEROD.   It makes no difference! I shall find it out.
       But one thing I must know from your own lips: 390
       Whether and how I shall defend myself.
MARIAMNE.   Whether—
HEROD.   Oh Mariamne, do not ask!
       You know how strong the bond that holds me to you,
       You know that every day but makes it stronger,
       And you must surely realize, I now   395
       Can not fight for myself if you do not
       Assure me that your heart still beats for me!
       Oh tell me whether ardently or coldly,
       Then I will tell you whether Antony
       Will call me brother, or perhaps condemn   400
       Me to the subterranean dungeon where
       Jugurtha died the death of slow starvation!
       Why are you silent? Speak! For this confession
       Does not, I feel, beseem a king; he should
       Not be subjected to the common lot   405
       Of man, should not be bound within himself
       To any being that's outside of him,
       He should be bound to God alone, and I
       Am not! When you a year ago lay sick
       And at the point of death, I had the thought   410
       That I would kill myself. I could not bear
       To live if you were dead—you know this now,
       So know one other thing! If ever I
       Myself lay dying I could even do
       What you expect Salome would, prepare   415

ACT I, SCENE 3

    A poison in your wine and give it to you,
    So I should still be sure of you in death!
MARIAMNE. If you did that, you would no doubt recover!
HEROD. Oh no! For I would share this poison with you!   420
    But tell me whether you could e'er forgive
    Such an excess of love as that would be!
MARIAMNE. If after drinking such a drink I still
    Had only breath enough for one last word,
    Then I would curse you with that final word.
    (aside) Yes, all the more, the more I'm sure that I   425
    Could reach out for the dagger in my grief
    To kill myself if death should call you hence:
    That one can do, not have it done to him!
HEROD. In this last night a fire consumed a woman
    With her dead husband; and although they tried   430
    To save her, she resisted. You probably
    Despise this woman then?
MARIAMNE.   Who says I do?
    She was not forced to be a sacrifice,
    She sacrificed herself and thus she proved
    The man meant more to her than all the world.   435
HEROD. And you? And I?
MARIAMNE.   If in yourself you feel
    That you mean more to me than all the world,
    What else is there to keep me in the world?
HEROD. The world! The world still has so many kings
    And there is none among them who would not   440
    Be glad to share his throne with you, would not
    Desert his bride, cast out his wife for you,
    And had the wedding been the night before!
MARIAMNE. Is Cleopatra dead, that you speak so?
HEROD. You are so beautiful, whoever sees you   445
    Has to believe in immortality,
    Of which the Pharisees so glibly speak,
    For none believes your image ever could
    Die out in him; so beautiful I should
    Not be surprised if suddenly the mountains   450
    Provided me a metal to adorn you
    More precious far then even gold or silver,
    A metal kept reserved until you came;
    So beautiful that—Ah, to know you'll die
    From love, the moment that another dies,   455
    To hasten after him who went before,
    To mingle in that sphere in which one is
    And yet is not, for so I think of it,
    As your last breath and his last breath together—
    That would be worth a voluntary death,   460
    Would mean to find a bliss beyond the grave

Where horror dwells: oh, may I, Mariamne,
Perhaps still hope for this, or must I fear
That you—for Antony has asked about you!
MARIAMNE. One does not ask a promissory note 465
On deeds, much less on pain and sacrifice,
Such as despair, I feel, may bring, but which
Love never can demand!
HEROD. Farewell!
MARIAMNE. Farewell!
I know you will return; for He alone 470
(pointing to Heaven)
Decrees that you shall die!
HEROD. So little fear?
MARIAMNE. So great assurance!
HEROD. Love is ever anxious!
It trembles even in the hero's breast!
MARIAMNE. Mine trembles not at all!
HEROD. You do not tremble!
MARIAMNE. Now I begin! If you can trust no more
Since you contrived my brother's—Then alas 475
For me, and you!
HEROD. You do not give your word,
Your simple word, when I had hoped to have
A vow from you; on what shall I depend?
MARIAMNE. And if I made it, what is your assurance
That I would keep it? Only I myself, 480
My nature as you know it. So I think,
Since you must end with hope and trust in me,
You might as well begin with both of them!
Go! I can not do otherwise! Not yet! *(exit)*

SCENE 4

HEROD. Not yet! Tomorrow or some other day!— 485
She plans to do me favors after death!
A wife speaks so? Of course I know that often
When I had called her beautiful, she twisted
Her face awry till she no longer was,
I know she can not weep, and spasms are 490
For her what tears for others! I also know
She quarreled with her brother not so long
Before he met his death while in the bath
And afterwards would not be reconciled;
Yes, more than that, when he already was 495
A corpse, a gift was brought from him which he
Had bought for her while on his way to bathe.
Yet does a wife speak so, and at the moment
The man she loves, or surely is at least

ACT I, SCENE 5

Supposed to love — — She is not turning back, 500
As once, when I — — She left no scarf behind
As pretext — — No, she can endure to have
Me leave with this impression — — Very well!
To Alexandria—the grave—no matter!
But one thing first! One! Earth and Heaven listen! 505
You made no vow to me, but I make one
To you: I place you now beneath the sword!
If Antony puts me to death for you,—
And for your mother's sake he will not do it!—
He but deceives himself; though it is doubtful 510
Whether the clothes that cover me at death
Will follow to the grave, because a thief
May rob my corpse, yet you shall follow me!
That is my vow! If I do not return,
You perish! That command I leave behind! 515
Command! But that presents a vexing problem;
How to assure myself obedience
When I am feared no more? Oh, someone will
Be found, I think, who has good cause to be
In fear of her! 520

SCENE 5

SERVANT.　　　　　　Your brother-in-law!
HEROD.　　　　　　　　　　　Is welcome!
　That is my man! I will give him my sword
　And then by working on his cowardice
　Incite his courage to the point of using it!
JOSEPH *(enters)*. I hear you think of setting out at once
　For Alexandria. I wish Godspeed! 525
HEROD. I leave at once. May be, not to return.
JOSEPH. You fear that you will not return?
HEROD.　　　　　　　　　　　　　I might not!
JOSEPH. You never talked like this before!
HEROD.　　　　　　　　　　　　　Then be
　Assured, things never looked so bad for me!
JOSEPH. If you are losing heart— 530
HEROD.　　　　　　　　But I am not,
　For I shall bear whatever comes, but hope
　Is gone that any good may come of it.
JOSEPH. I only wish that I had been quite blind
　And never had laid bare the secret plans
　Of Alexandra! 535
HEROD.　　　　That I can believe!
JOSEPH. For if I never had found out that she
　Had had Aristobulus' portrait painted
　Quite secretly for Antony, and if

        I had not learned that she sent messages
        To Cleopatra, and then last of all
        I had not seized the coffin in the harbor,
        Which hid her son and her, and stopped their flight
        When it had scarce begun—
HEROD.   Then she would have
        Nothing to thank you for, and you could calmly
        Stand by and see her daughter on the throne,
        Which Mariamne, daring Maccabee,
        Will surely seize if I do not return,
        And if no other seizes it before her.
JOSEPH. I do not mean that. I mean, many things
        Would never have been done!
HEROD.   Yes, that is right!
        But other things would have occurred instead.
        That makes no difference—You recounted much,
        One thing you have forgotten!
JOSEPH.   What is that?
HEROD. You too were in the bath when he—
JOSEPH.   I was!
HEROD. You wrestled with him too?
JOSEPH.   At first I did.
HEROD. Well then!
JOSEPH.   The dizzy spell had not yet seized him
        While I was with him, if it had come on,
        I would have rescued him, or else he would
        Have pulled me down with him beneath the waves.
HEROD. I have no doubt of that. But you must know
        That no one who was there speaks otherwise,
        And since an evil chance decreed that you
        Not only went into the water with him
        But wrestled with him too—
JOSEPH.   Why do you stop?
HEROD. My Joseph, you and I, the two of us,
        We are accused!
JOSEPH.   I too?
HEROD.   You are not only
        My brother-in-law, you are my friend as well!
JOSEPH. I hope I am!
HEROD.   Oh had you never been!
        Had I, like Saul, but thrown the spear at you
        And you could prove it by your gaping wounds,
        It would be better for you, then this slander
        Would not have found a willing ear, nor would
        You be beheaded for a bloody deed
        You never did commit!
JOSEPH.   What, I? Beheaded?
HEROD. That is your lot if I do not return

ACT I, SCENE 5

    And Mariamne—
JOSEPH.   I am innocent!
HEROD. What help is that? Appearances are bad!
    And even if they did believe, are not
    The many many services that you
    Have done for me, in Alexandra's eyes   580
    A proof of crimes against herself, will she
    Not think: If he had let me flee, then he
    Who now lies in the grave would be alive?
JOSEPH. True! True!
HEROD.   Can she not therefore with a sort
    Of right demand your life to pay for one   585
    That she believes she lost through act of yours,
    And will she not demand it of her daughter?
JOSEPH. Salome! This has come because I went
    To see the painter! Every year she wants
    A portrait of me!   590
HEROD.   I know how she loves you!
JOSEPH. Ah, if she loved me less it would be better!
    Would I have found Aristobulus' portrait,
    If I—Salome, you can now soon have
    My last one, but it will be headless!
HEROD.   Joseph,
    One must defend his head!   595
JOSEPH.   If you admit
    Your head is lost?
HEROD.   I do not quite do that,
    I still shall try to save it if I can,
    By putting it into the lion's jaws
    Quite voluntarily.
JOSEPH.   In that you once
    Succeeded when the Pharisees—   600
HEROD.   But now
    The case is worse, whatever comes to me,
    Your fate I leave with you in your own hands;
    You always were a man, be now a king!
    I hang the purple mantle round you, extend
    To you the scepter and the sword, so hold   605
    Them fast and give them back to me alone!
JOSEPH. But do I hear aright?
HEROD.   And to assure
    Possession of the throne and of your life,
    Kill Mariamne, if you ever hear
    That I am not returning.   610
JOSEPH.   Mariamne?
HEROD. She is the only bond that Alexandra
    Has with the people since the river drowned
    Her son, she is the brightly colored crest

        Rebellion will be sure to wear if it
        Rise up against you.   615
JOSEPH.   Yes, but Mariamne!
HEROD. You are astonished—I am not dissembling,
        And my advice is good, is good for you,
        What need for futher words? Yet it is not
        Alone for you—In plain words: I can not
        Endure the thought that any other ever—   620
        That would be bitterer than—she is proud
        I know—yet after death—an Antony—
        And then above all else this mother-in-law,
        Who will incite the dead against the dead — —
        You understand!   625
JOSEPH.   But—
HEROD.   Hear me to the end!
        She let me hope that she would kill herself
        With her own hand, if I—One has the right
        To have a debt collected?—One may even
        Use force to—What do you think?
JOSEPH.   I believe so!
HEROD. Then promise me that you will kill her, should she   630
        Not kill herself! Do not be overhasty,
        But do not wait too long! So go to her
        As soon as messengers, for I shall send them,
        Report to you that I am dead, and tell her;
        Then notice if she reaches for a dagger,   635
        If she does something else. You promise?
JOSEPH.   Yes!
HEROD. I will not have you swear an oath. There is
        No need to have one swear that he will crush
        A serpent that is threatening him with death.
        He does it of himself, if he is sane,   640
        Since he could leave off taking food and drink
        With much less danger than omitting this.
                      (Joseph moves nervously)
        I know you well! And I will recommend you,
        Tell Antony you are the only one
        Whom he may trust. That you will prove to him   645
        By showing him that even blood relations
        Are not too sacred for a sacrifice
        If there is need to stop a revolution.
        That is the explanation for the deed
        Which you must give him. Street rioting   650
        Will surely follow it, and you must tell him
        That rioting preceded it as well,
        Which only was subdued by killing her.
        And as concerns the people, they will shudder
        When they behold your bloody sword, and many   655

ACT I, SCENE 5

    Will say: I knew this man but half! And now—
JOSEPH. Until we meet again! Today is not
    The end! I know you will return, as always.
HEROD. A possibility, so one thing more! — — *(long pause)*
    I swore an oath just now concerning you!   660
              (he writes and seals)
    It is recorded here! Take this sealed sheet!
    You see it is addressed to—
JOSEPH.   To the hangman!
HEROD. And I shall keep what I have promised in it,
    If you should tell a tale about a king
    Perhaps, who gave—   665
JOSEPH.   Then give the order to me
    To take this sheet myself straight to the hangman! *(exit)*
HEROD *(alone)*. She lives beneath the sword, and that will spur me
    To do what I have never done, to bear
    What I have never borne, and comfort me
    If it is all in vain. And now, away!—*(exit)*   670

ACT II

Castle Zion.   Alexandra's rooms.

SCENE 1

Alexandra and Sameas.

ALEXANDRA. And now you know this!
SAMEAS.   I am not surprised!
   Nothing that Herod does surprises me!
   For one, who as a youth declares a war
   Against the Sanhedrin, with naked sword
   Steps up before his judge and gives him warning   675
   That he himself is hangman, and the hangman
   Will carry out no sentence on himself,
   He may as man — — Ah, I can see him yet,
   How he, undaunted by the high priest, leaned
   Against a column with his soldiers round him,   680
   Those soldiers who in chasing down the robbers
   Themselves had been transformed to robbers too,
   And calmly counted us all, one by one,
   As if he stood before a bed of thistles,
   And were deciding how to clear it out.   685
ALEXANDRA. Yes, yes. it was a moment made for him,
   On which he may quite well look back with pride!
   A youthful madcap, scarcely twenty years
   Of age, is summoned by the Sanhedrin,
   Because, in criminal excess of spirits,   690
   He has presumed to go against the law,
   Because he dared to carry out a sentence
   Of death which you had not as yet decreed.
   The widow of the dead man, with a curse,
   Has met him on the threshold, and within   695
   Sit all Jerusalem's old men and gray beards.
   Because he has not dressed in sackcloth, has
   Not strewed his head with ashes, you lose courage.
   You think no more of punishment for him,
   You do not even think of threatening him,   700
   You do not speak a word, he laughs and goes!
SAMEAS. I spoke!
ALEXANDRA.   It was too late!
SAMEAS.   If I had spoken
   Sooner, it would have been that much too soon,
   Respect for the high priest had kept me silent,
   The first word was for him, for me the last,   705
   He was the oldest there, the youngest I!
ALEXANDRA. Mere words! If then and there you Sanhedrists
   Had proved the simple courage of your duty,

ACT II, SCENE 1

    No greater courage would be needed now!
    But now see whether you — — Oh, you will find   710
    Some other good excuse, I know! If you
    Are not inclined to fight with him—in fact,
    It would be venturesome and I advise
    Against it—then you only need to fight
    With lions or with tigers when he orders.   715
SAMEAS. What's that?
ALEXANDRA.   You know the gladiatorial combats,
    The Roman games?
SAMEAS.   Praise God, I know them not!
    I think it is a gain to know what Moses
    Tells us about the Gentiles, nothing else;
    I close my eyes quite tightly every time   720
    A Roman soldier meets me on the street,
    And I still bless my father in his grave
    That he had never taught their tongue to me.
ALEXANDRA. You do not know they bring wild animals
    To Rome, which they have sent from Africa   725
    By hundreds?
SAMEAS.   No, I had not heard of that.
ALEXANDRA. That in the stone arena there they drive
    Them all together, that they then send in
    Their slaves to them, who have to fight with them
    Till men or beasts are dead, while they themselves   730
    Sit round them in the amphitheater
    And shout with joy when mortal wounds are gaping,
    And when the bright red blood spurts on the sand?
SAMEAS. The wildest of my dreams has never shown
    Me that, and yet it fills my soul with joy   735
    To learn of it, it is well suited to them!
            (with hands upraised)
    Lord, Thou are great! Though Thou dost grant the Gentile
    The right to life, yet he must pay Thee tribute,
    A fearful tribute for it too, for he
    Is punished by the very way he lives it!—   740
    How I should like to see those games!
ALEXANDRA.   Your wish
    Shall be fulfilled when Herod has returned,
    He thinks of introducing them!
SAMEAS.   Oh, never!
ALEXANDRA. That's what I said! And why not? For we have
    Lions a plenty! And the mountain herdsman   745
    Rejoices if their number but grows less,
    For that will save him many cows and calves.
SAMEAS. But quite aside from all the rest, where would
    He find the fighters? There are no slaves with us,
    Who owe him service even unto death.   750

ALEXANDRA. The first—I see before me!
SAMEAS. What?
ALEXANDRA. Of course!
    You will distort your face as you do now,
    Perhaps will even tightly clench your fists,
    Will roll your eyes and gnash your teeth with rage
    When you shall live to see the day on which   755
    He dedicates the heathenish arena
    As festively as Solomon the Temple.
    All that will not escape him, as reward
    He will command you by a sign to enter
    And show the people there what you can do,   760
    When you are thus confronted with a lion
    That has been kept from food for many days.
    For since we have no slaves, the criminals
    Deserving death will have to take their place,
    And who then is deserving death, if he   765
    Is not, who openly defies the King!
SAMEAS. He could—
ALEXANDRA. Oh, do not doubt! It would be bad
    If they should take his head from him too soon,
    Then there would die with him such mighty plans
    As even Pompey, who with impious boldness   770
    Once dared to penetrate the Inner Temple,
    Perhaps—
SAMEAS *(bursting out)*. Oh Antony, if you destroy him,
    Then for a whole year long I will not curse you,
    And if you do not—well then, we are ready!
ALEXANDRA. He thinks that if our people were intended   775
    To keep from mixing with the others, God would
    Have given us the world all for ourselves!
SAMEAS. Does he think that?
ALEXANDRA. Since that is not the case,
    He thinks that there is need to break the bars,
    Which separate us still from all the rest,   780
    As dykes cut stagnant pools off from the sea.
    And that could happen, if we would adapt
    Ourselves to them in usage and in customs.
SAMEAS. In usage—*(to Heaven)* Lord! If I am not to go
    Completely mad, show me how he will die!   785
    Show me the death that borrows all the horrors
    From every other death, and then proclaim
    To me, it is for Herod this is done!
ALEXANDRA. Then be yourself death's angel!
SAMEAS. For myself,
    If not for him! I swear! I will prevent   790
    This outrage or will punish my own weakness
    And kill myself *(with a motion toward his breast)*

ACT II, SCENE 1

               before the day arrives
  Which is besmirched by such abomination!
  That oath compels me to commit a crime
  If I can not perform heroic deeds;   795
  What man is there who ever swore a greater?
ALEXANDRA. Good! But do not forget, if your own arm's
  Not strong enough to overcome the foe,
  Do not reject with scorn the arms of others!
SAMEAS. These others?   800
ALEXANDRA.   You can arm them easily!
SAMEAS. Explain your words!
ALEXANDRA.   Who gave the royal crown
  To Herod?
SAMEAS.   Antony! Who else than he?
ALEXANDRA. Why did he do that?
SAMEAS.   Because he liked him!
  Or merely this, because we did not like him!
  When has a Gentile had a better reason?   805
ALEXANDRA. Another thing! What keeps him on the throne?
SAMEAS. The people's blessing, no! Perhaps its curse!
  Well, who can say?
ALEXANDRA.   Why I! The trick alone
  Of sending in the tribute we must pay
  The Romans every year, before it's due,   810
  And even freely doubling it unasked,
  If somewhere a new war has broken out.
  The Roman wants our money, nothing more,
  He lets us keep our ancient faith, our God,
  And he would even honor Him with us,   815
  Grant Him that place upon the Capitol
  Beside his Jupiter and Ops and Isis,
  Which is unoccupied until today,
  If He, like them, were only made of stone.
SAMEAS. If that is so, and I regret to say   820
  It is, what do you hope from Antony?
  In this respect, as you yourself have said,
  There's nothing Herod leaves undone. Just now—
  I saw him go! The back of one mule broke
  Before it even reached the city gate!   825
  For every drop of blood within his veins
  He offers him an ounce of gold; do you
  Believe he will reject the gold for you?
ALEXANDRA. Of course not, if I acted for myself!
  But Cleopatra works in my behalf   830
  And Mariamne helps me too, I hope.
  You are surprised? I do not mean in person,
  She is more apt herself to work against me,
  But through her portrait, and not even that,

No, through another which resembles her. 835
For as the forest shelters not alone
The lion but his foe the tiger too,
There nestles also in this Roman's heart
A swarming serpent-brood of fiery passions
Which struggle with each other for control, 840
And if now Herod builds upon the first,
Then I build on the second, and I think
The second one is stronger than the first.
SAMEAS. You are—
ALEXANDRA. No Hyrcanus, although his daughter!
But lest you should misjudge what I have done, 845
Know this: I am no Mariamne either!
If Antony destroys the husband, who
Possesses her, to clear the way to her:
She still is mistress of herself and can
Entrench herself behind her widow's veil. 850
But I am certain of one thing: already
His hand is on his sword, and if he has
Not drawn it, only this consideration
Has really held him back: the Romans think
This lucky soldier Herod is the ring 855
Of iron holding things together here.
Just bring the proof the opposite is true,
Stir up revolt, disturb this lazy peace,
Then he will draw it!
SAMEAS. That will be quite easy!
In thought the people have already slain him 860
And it is said—
ALEXANDRA. So put your seal upon it,
And quickly then disclose his testament!
You know its contents now, the Roman games
Stand first in it, and if each one believes
He will receive a hundred lashes less 865
By Herod's death, or miss the martyr's cross,
Then each one thinks, what he is right in thinking.
For Israel is facing things so terrible,
That it may force from many hearts the wish
Of utter desperation, that the Red Sea 870
Had swallowed all the people, all twelve tribes
Of Israel, and Moses first of all.
SAMEAS. I go! Before the noontide comes—
ALEXANDRA. I know
What you can do when you put sackcloth on
And, shouting woe! alas! move through the streets 875
As if your forebear Jonah were among us.
And you will learn that it is very useful
To go sometimes to see the fisherman,

ACT II, SCENE 2   33

    And eat that humble tradesman's food that he
    Permits himself because no one has bought it.   880
SAMEAS. And you yourself will learn, we Pharisees
    Have not forgotten the disgrace we suffered,
    As you seem to believe. So listen now
    To something you were not supposed to learn
    Until it happened: we are sworn long since   885
    Against him, all Judea's undermined
    And in Jerusalem, so you will see
    How firmly we can count upon the people,
    There even is a blind man in our league.
ALEXANDRA. What use is he?   890
SAMEAS.   Why none! And that he knows!
    But yet he is so filled with hate and anger,
    That he would rather share the undertaking
    With us and die, than still continue living
    In such a world, if it should not succeed.
    I think we may consider this a sign. *(exit)*   895

SCENE 2

ALEXANDRA *(alone)*. In thought the people have already slain him!
    I know! I know! And I can see by that
    How much they wish he never will return.
    How fortunate that as he left the swarm
    Of locusts hid him from our sight, for that's   900
    An omen that they do not wish in vain.
    And it is possible that even now
    He is beheaded.—No, speak as you think,
    No Pharisee is lurking at the door!
    And Antony is Antony, I know,   905
    He is a Roman too, and Romans form
    Their judgments slowly, execute them swiftly.
    He may now be a prisoner, although
    Not yet in prison! If one uses that,
    It can lead further. Therefore it is good   910
    If insurrection comes, although I know
    What insurrection means, no less I know
    What consequences it will have if he
    Returns in spite of all. If! That can happen,
    So weigh it well! Before he left, he sent   915
    A severed head as parting gift to you.
    That shows—Fie! I am talking like my father!
    That shows me he is swift as tyrants are,
    And also that he aims to frighten me.
    The first I knew long since, the other shall not 920
    Succeed! And if the very worst should come,
    If everything I try should fail, if he

Should dare the worst in spite of his strong love
For Mariamne, which will rather mount
Than fall, and will protect me if she will— 925
What of it? I have ventured all for vengeance,
In death it would be vengeance still, on him
Who did it and on her who let it happen.
The people, even Rome itself, would not
Look on at it with patience. As for me, 930
I should be better suited to my forebears
If death for me should be a bloody one!
Did not the great-grandfathers of my race,
The great-grandmothers too, did not the most
Of them go to the grave without their heads 935
Because they would not bow them? I should share
Their lot with them, what more then would it be?

SCENE 3

Mariamne enters.

ALEXANDRA *(aside).*
She comes! Yes, if she could be turned from him
And could be moved to follow me to Rome,
Then—But, she hates him and she loves him too! 940
Shall I still dare a last attack? So be it!
   (she hastens up to Mariamne)
You seek for comfort where it can be found!
Come to my heart!
MARIAMNE.   Comfort?
ALEXANDRA.   You feel no need?
I have misjudged you then! But I had reasons
For thinking you the sort of wife you are not, 945
And what I heard was slander!
MARIAMNE.   What you heard?
ALEXANDRA. They told me of embraces and of kisses
You gave your fratricidal husband right
After the murder—Do forgive, I should
Not have believed it. 950
MARIAMNE.   No?
ALEXANDRA.   No, never, never!
For more than one good reason! Even if
You could have turned so heartlessly aside,
Refused to give your brother's bloody shade
A sister's offering of revenge, which you
Could take, not by a Judith's sword, nor yet 955
By Rahab's nail, but merely by a twist
Of lip or silent crossing of your arms,
And should have taken for the dead man's sake:
The murderer himself would not have dared

ACT II, SCENE 3

    Approach, for you resemble so the dead man,   960
    You would have seemed to him too like the corpse,
    Aristobulus' corpse, made up with rouge.
    He would have turned away from you and shuddered.
MARIAMNE. He did not do the one, nor I the other!
ALEXANDRA. Then be—But no! Perhaps some doubt remained   965
    As to his guilt. Do you want proof of it?
MARIAMNE. I need no proof!
ALEXANDRA.   You—
MARIAMNE.   It is not important!
ALEXANDRA. Then—But I hold the curse back even now,
    For you are laden with another one!
    You still are bound in fetters by a love   970
    Which never brought you honor.
MARIAMNE.   But I thought,
    I did not choose my husband for myself,
    I but submitted to the lot which you
    And Hyrcanus deliberately imposed
    On me, the grandchild and the daughter.   975
ALEXANDRA.   Not I
    But my faint-hearted father planned the marriage.
MARIAMNE. Then what he did displeased you?
ALEXANDRA.   No, it did not!
    For then I would have fled with you before—
    A refuge had been offered me in Egypt.
    I only say that he evolved the plan,   980
    The first of all our high priests lacking courage;
    I merely fought the feeling of aversion
    With which I heard the plan at first. But still
    I did it, for I liked the coward's deal
    On second thought, and gave the pearl of Zion   985
    For Edom's sword, when he insisted on it!
    Yes, if the serpent had been poisonous
    That at the time had bitten Cleopatra,
    Or if Mark Antony, when on his journey,
    Had only come this way, why then I would   990
    Have answered no! As 'twas, I answered yes!
MARIAMNE. And yet—
ALEXANDRA.   I had expected that you would
    Not merely waste the purchase price, I hoped
    That you would ask of Herod—
MARIAMNE.   Oh, I know!
    I should have made him pay for every kiss   995
    By granting me a head that you disliked,
    And finally when no one more defied you
    Save only he himself, have driven him
    To suicide, or if that did not work,
    On some still night I should have craftily   1000

      Repeated Judith's sneaking deed on him;
      That would have made you proud to call me daughter!
ALEXANDRA. Much prouder, I do not deny, than now.
MARIAMNE. But I preferred to be a wife to him   1005
      To whom you married me, for love of him
      Forget I was a Maccabee, as he
      Forgot that he was king for love of me.
ALEXANDRA. In Jericho, however, you again
      Remembered it, or so it seemed, at least
      You were the first who openly accused him   1010
      While I myself held back with my complaint,
      To test you. Am I right?
MARIAMNE.   In Jericho
      The terrible event confused me so,
      It came too suddenly, from meal to bath,
      From bath to grave, a brother, I admit   1015
      My brain reeled! If, however, stubborn and
      Suspicious, I closed my door to king and husband,
      I'm sorry now and can forgive myself
      Only because it happened as in fever!
ALEXANDRA. In fever!
MARIAMNE *(half to herself)*. I would not have done it either   1020
      If he had not worn mourning when he came!
      In red, in deep dark red, I could have seen him,
      But—
ALEXANDRA. Yes, he found it quickly! He had ordered
      It in advance, as other murderers
      Draw water, possibly, before they murder—   1025
MARIAMNE. Mother, do not forget!
ALEXANDRA.   What? That you are
      The murderer's wife? That's something you've become,
      And only are as long as you desire,
      Perhaps right now, who knows! you're that no longer;
      But yet you always were the dead man's sister   1030
      And that you will remain, you even still
      Will be, if you—you seem inclined to do it—
      Should shout into his grave: It serves you right!
MARIAMNE. I owe respect to you, I should not like
      To do it violence and, therefore, stop!   1035
      For otherwise I could—
ALEXANDRA.   What?
MARIAMNE.   Ask myself
      Who is more guilty of it, whether it's
      The man who did the deed because he had to
      Or she who drove him to it! Let the dead rest!
ALEXANDRA. Then speak to one who did not give him birth!   1040
      I carried him beneath my heart, and must
      Avenge him, since I can not waken him,

ACT II, SCENE 3

    That he avenge himself!
MARIAMNE.   Avenge him then,
    Avenge him on yourself! You know full well
    That as high priest, surrounded and acclaimed   1045
    So by the mob, his head turned by the honor,
    Not as the heedless youth Aristobulus,
    He brought upon himself the thing that happened.
    Now tell me who it was that stirred him up
    And made him lose his self-complacency!   1050
    He had no lack of gaily colored clothes,
    That so attract the eyes of pretty girls,
    He had no need of more to make him happy.
    What need had he of Aaron's priestly mantle,
    Which you draped round him as an added glory?   1055
    He had himself no other thought about it
    Than this: Is it becoming to me? Others,
    However, from the moment that he donned it,
    Thought him the second head of Israel
    And you soon managed so to turn his head   1060
    He thought himself the first and only one!
ALEXANDRA. You slander him and me.
MARIAMNE.   Oh no, I do not!
    If this gay youth who seemed to have been born
    To be the first completely happy person,
    If he so quickly met a gloomy fate,   1065
    And if the man who makes all other men
    Rank cowards if he draws his sword, if he—
    I do not know he did it, but I fear it;
    Then lust for power and ambition are
    To blame, not the ambition of the dead man   1070
    And not the lust for power of the King!
    To lay the blame on you would not be seemly;
    I do not ask that you should shed a single
    Repentant tear because you sent a ghost,
    A bloody ghost, into our wedding chamber,   1075
    Although we two no longer are alone,
    And now the third disturbs my mind so much
    That I am silent when I ought to speak
    And speak when it were better to be silent.
    I will not even try to quench your zeal   1080
    For vengeance, will not ask what you avenge,
    Whether it is your plans or is your son:
    Do what you will, go on, or call a halt,
    But be assured that if you strike at Herod
    You strike at Mariamne too; the oath   1085
    That I refused, when he demanded it
    On parting, I will swear it now: I die,
    If he should die. So act and say no more!

ALEXANDRA. Then die! And now! For—
MARIAMNE.   Oh, I understand you!
   And that is why you thought I needed comfort?   1090
   Oh no! You're wrong! I do not feel alarm
   If menial mobs, which only tolerate
   The chosen few because they're human, mortal,
   Already have put him to death with words.
   What else is there a slave can do, whene'er   1095
   A king goes by in regal pomp and splendor,
   Than say: His turn will surely come, like mine!
   I do not grudge him that! and if he moves
   A battlefield with many graves up close
   Beside the throne, I quite approve of that,   1100
   It stifles envy! Yet my heart tells me
   That Herod lives and will live. Death must cast
   A shadow, it falls here, inside!

SCENE 4

SERVANT.   The Viceroy!
ALEXANDRA. And surely armed, just as he always is,
   Whenever he comes to see us, since he failed   1105
   To dupe us by the use of flattery,
   As seemed to be his aim when first he came.
   Do you know that Salome almost died
   Of jealousy of you?
MARIAMNE.   She still is jealous!
   For constantly, when she is near, I tell him   1110
   The worst things, smiling intimately,
   And since she never wearies of her spying,
   I do not weary either, plaguing her
   Because she is so foolish!
                    Joseph enters.
ALEXANDRA *(pointing to his weapons).* See!
MARIAMNE.   Oh let him!
   His wife demands it so that she can dream   1115
   She has a valiant and courageous husband.
ALEXANDRA *(to Joseph).*
   I am still here, you see!
JOSEPH.   A strange reception!
ALEXANDRA. My son is still here too! He has again
   Concealed himself within a dead man's coffin.
   If you will drive him forth, I will forgive you   1120
   For having done it once before unbidden.
   But this time you must seek the coffin, not
   On any ship that sails the sea to Egypt,
   But deep within the bowels of the earth!
JOSEPH. I am not one who can awake the dead!   1125

ACT II, SCENE 4

ALEXANDRA *(scornfully to Mariamne).*
    How true! For then you would have gone to Egypt
    To help your master when he kneels and pleads
    And that does not protect him from the axe—
MARIAMNE. He kneel and plead!
JOSEPH *(to Mariamne).*   And I can show you how!   1130
    "I am accused of this!" Yes, I admit it.
    "But not of this!" I add it right at once
    So that you know it all! He'll do it so.
ALEXANDRA. You boast for him?
JOSEPH.   He did that once before!
    I stood beside him, when the Pharisees
    Had planned to file a charge with Antony.   1135
    He hastened on to camp ahead of them
    Just as he was, told it himself instead,
    And when they came, repeating all the charge,
    Enlarging point by point, he said: Now speak!
    Have I omitted anything or not?   1140
    You know the end, how many an accuser
    Then lost his stubborn head for not retracting;
    He had the Roman's favor when he left.
ALEXANDRA. The two were younger then than they are now.
    The arrogance of Herod pleased the other,   1145
    And all the more, since others bore the cost
    Not he himself. The Pharisee whose tongue
    Is always preaching of revolt 'gainst Rome,
    Can he be anything? Whoever plucks
    His beard for him, reduces his esteem!   1150
    Thus Antony did think and laugh, I doubt
    That he will let that happen to himself!
JOSEPH. You speak as if you wished—
ALEXANDRA.   Whether we wish
    Alike or not is no concern of yours!
    Hold your wish fast! For you it is important   1155
    That he return!
JOSEPH.   You think so? If for me,
    Then too for you!
ALEXANDRA.   I know no reason why!
    There was an Alexandra once before
    Who came to wear a crown in Israel,
    Who seized it when no king was wearing it   1160
    And did not leave it for a thief to steal.
    By God, there soon shall be a second one
    If there are really *(to Mariamne)* Maccabean women
    Who keep their childish oaths!
JOSEPH *(listening).*   Yes, it is true!
    There really was once such an Alexandra,   1165
    But if one will attain her goal, he'll have

  To follow her example to the full,
  Not merely half. She reconciled herself
  With all her foes when once she took the throne,
  Now no one feared her more but only hoped,   1170
  No wonder that she sat secure till death!
MARIAMNE. That is deplorable! Why have a scepter,
  If not to satisfy both love and hate?
  A twig's enough to scare away the flies!
JOSEPH. How true! *(to Alexandra)* And you?   1175
ALEXANDRA.   She never saw in dreams
  The father of her race, the mighty Judas,
  Else she would not have feared a single foe,
  For even from the grave he guards his children,
  Because he cannot die in any heart.
  How should he die! No one can ever pray,   1180
  Who does not have to say: It's due to him
  That I may kneel before my God and not
  Before a god of wood or stone or bronze!
JOSEPH *(aside)*. The King was right! I must commit the deed,
  Put both to death or suffer death myself.   1185
  I have to put the crown upon my head
  If I would save it from the hangman's axe.
  A world of hate stares at me here! So be it!
  They have pronounced the sentence on themselves;
  Now for the last time I have tested them,   1190
  And if his messenger were here, I would
  This very moment do it without mercy!
  My preparations are already made.

SCENE 5

SERVANT. The Captain Titus asks an audience!
JOSEPH. At once. *(He is about to go)*   1195
ALEXANDRA.   And why not here?
SERVANT.   He's here already!
TITUS *(enters; secretly to Joseph)*.
  The thing you feared is happening, the people
  Are in revolt!
JOSEPH.   Then do what I commanded,
  Draw up your cohorts and advance at once!
TITUS. That is already done. I come to ask:
  Do you want prisoners or only dead men?   1200
  My eagle merely seizes, or it mangles,
  And you must know which method suits you better.
JOSEPH. No blood must flow!
TITUS.   Good! I shall then move in
  Before the stoning starts, but otherwise
  I should delay!   1205

ACT II, SCENE 5

JOSEPH.   Did you see Sameas?
TITUS. The Pharisee who one time almost crashed
  His head against my shield because he shuts
  His eyes each time he catches sight of me?
  I saw him, to be sure!
JOSEPH.   And how? Speak loudly!
TITUS. With thousands round him in the open market   1210
  And loudly cursing Herod!
JOSEPH *(to Alexandra)*.   Sameas
  Just left you! It was not an hour ago!
ALEXANDRA. You saw?
TITUS *(to Joseph)*. You'll come yourself?
JOSEPH.   When I can!
  And in the meantime—
TITUS.   I am leaving! *(turns to go)*
ALEXANDRA *(calls him back)*.   Captain!
  Why did you take away our guard?   1215
MARIAMNE.   The guard
  Has gone?
ALEXANDRA. Yes, yesterday!
JOSEPH.   I ordered it!
TITUS. Because the King told me before he went:
  This is the man who knows just what I want,
  What he commands, that I command myself! *(exit)*
ALEXANDRA *(to Joseph)*.
  And you!   1220
JOSEPH. I thought that Judas Maccabaeus
  Was guard enough for you and for your daughter.
  And furthermore you hear how things are going:
  I need the soldiers elsewhere! *(aside)* If the Romans
  Were near, it might not be successful! Today
  I sent the Galileans!   1225
ALEXANDRA *(to Mariamne)*. Do you still
  Think my suspicion false?
MARIAMNE.   I do not know,
  But it infects me now. I find this strange!
  Although—If spears came flying from the wall
  They would not come more unexpectedly!
ALEXANDRA. Two dagger thrusts would clear the way for him;   1230
  For if there are no Maccabees alive,
  Then the Herodians will claim the throne.
MARIAMNE. I should still laugh at you, were only
  Salome not his wife!—But by my brother,
  Her head is mine! And I will say to Herod: 1235
  As you give me revenge on her, just so
  You love me! For it must be she, not he!
ALEXANDRA. Do not rejoice too soon! First we must act,
  And this revolt can serve our purpose well!

MARIAMNE. I will not be involved in this revolt,   1240
   Because, if Herod does return, I have
   Nothing to fear, and if he does not come,
   Then I will welcome death in any form!
ALEXANDRA. I'm going! *(starts to leave)*
JOSEPH *(stepping in her way)*. Where?
ALEXANDRA.   Up to the parapet
   For now, and after that where I may please!   1245
JOSEPH. The way up to the parapet is open!
   The fortress closed!
ALEXANDRA.   So we are prisoners?
JOSEPH. Until the time when peace has been restored,
   I must request you—
ALEXANDRA.   Are you not presuming?
JOSEPH. A stone is blind, a Roman javelin too,   1250
   They both may hit what they are not supposed to,
   So one must keep out of the way of them!
ALEXANDRA *(to Mariamne)*.
   Then I shall go and try to tell my friends
   Somehow by signs how matters stand with us.
MARIAMNE. By signs—your friends—oh mother, mother! So   1255
   It really is yourself and not the people?
   I hope you are not digging your own grave!
         (Alexandra starts to go)
JOSEPH. With your permission I shall send along
   My man-at-arms. Philo!
ALEXANDRA.   Open war then?
   (Philo enters; Joseph speaks to him in low tones, then aloud)
JOSEPH. You understand?   1260
PHILO.   Yes!
JOSEPH.   As a last resort!
PHILO. I am to watch, and then—
JOSEPH.   Your head is pawn!
   (aside) It seems that Herod's spirit is within me!
ALEXANDRA *(aside)*. But yet I go! Perhaps this man-at-arms,
   Although a Galilean, may be won!
   I can but try! *(exit; Philo follows her)*   1265
JOSEPH *(aside)*. There is no other way
   However much it throws suspicion on me,
   For the revolt drives me to take this step,
   I do not dare lose sight of her, unless
   I want to make the deed impossible;
   His messenger may come at any hour!   1270
   I gave up long ago expecting Herod.
MARIAMNE. And when did Herod die?
JOSEPH.   When did he die?
MARIAMNE. And how? You ought to know, you risk so much!
JOSEPH. What am I risking then? You ask a riddle!

MARIAMNE. Nothing, if you believe I shall not find 1275
  Protection when the Romans hear my life
  Is threatened, everything if you are wrong.
JOSEPH. And who is threatening your life?
MARIAMNE.   You ask?
  You!
JOSEPH.   I?
MARIAMNE.   And can you swear the opposite?
  By your child's head! Well, can you?—You are silent! 1280
JOSEPH. You have no right to ask an oath of me.
MARIAMNE. One so accused denies it of himself.
  Alas for you if Herod now returns!
  Two things I have to say before I kiss him,
  The one is, that you planned to murder me, 1285
  The other, what I swore; now judge yourself
  What fate is waiting for you when he comes!
JOSEPH. What did you swear? If it shall frighten me,
  Then I must know it.
MARIAMNE.   Let it be your curse!
  That I will kill myself with my own hand 1290
  If he—Ah! Now you think: Had I but known that!
  Why then I should have paid no heed at all
  To a cold greeting, should have gone ahead
  As I began and now all would be well!—
  You were a very different man at first! 1295
JOSEPH. I have no thing to fear!
MARIAMNE.   Because you think
  It is impossible that he return!
  Who knows! And if! Then I shall keep my oath,
  But not until I am avenged on you,
  Till I have so avenged myself—yes, tremble— 1300
  As he would have avenged me! Draw your sword
  At once! Draw it! You dare not? I believe it!
  However you may guard me, I shall find
  A way to Captain Titus I am sure!
  Your game is lost, since I have found it out. 1305
JOSEPH *(aside)*. True!
      (to Mariamne) I shall hold you to your word! You will
  Avenge yourself as Herod would avenge you!
  You have vowed that to me! Do not forget it!
MARIAMNE. Thus madness speaks! That Herod loves me
  Far more than I can love myself, no one 1310
  Will doubt, Salome even will not doubt it,
  That tricky wife of yours, not even if
  She hate me doubly for it, even if
  She be the one who for revenge has put
  The ugly thought of murder in your head! 1315
  That the idea comes from her, I know,

  And I will smite her so it hurts, her grief
  For you shall be my last real joy on earth!
JOSEPH. Though wrong, it matters not! I have your word!
MARIAMNE. You keep repeating it? Accursed man,   1320
  What fearful turmoil of dark thoughts you wake
  In me, and what suspicions in my breast!
  You speak as if King Herod had himself
  Picked you as sacrificial priest and me
  As victim. Is it so? As he took leave   1325
  He dropped a vague dark hint, I think of it
  With horror. Answer!
JOSEPH.   I shall answer you
  As soon as necessary, when I know
  That he—
MARIAMNE. No longer can expose your lies,
  When you with evil cowardice accuse him   1330
  Of the most terrible and monstrous thing
  Only to clear yourself from my suspicions?
  I tell you, I will hear you only now,
  When he, perhaps before you even finish,
  May enter at the door and strike you down!   1335
  Keep silent then forever, or speak now!
JOSEPH. And if it were? I do not say it is!
  But if it were? What else then would it be
  Than confirmation of the things you feel,
  Than proof that he loves you, as no man yet   1340
  Has ever loved his wife?
MARIAMNE.   What did you say?
  It seems to me I heard that once before!
JOSEPH. I thought that it would only flatter you
  If death were not one half as bitter for him
  As is the thought of leaving—   1345
MARIAMNE.   What the wager,
  That I myself can finish that for you!
  As is the thought of leaving me behind
  Within a world where Antony still lives!
JOSEPH. Well, yes! I do not say that he said that—
MARIAMNE. He said it! He said— Oh, what did he not say!   1350
  If he would only come!
JOSEPH.   But Mariamne!—
  (aside) I have become entangled! Yet I did
  No more than what I had to! But I fear
  That he—I see the dead Aristobulus.
  Accursed be the deed that throws a shadow   1355
  Before it's even done!
MARIAMNE.   So it was more
  Than merely empty bubbles in my brain,
  As may sometimes develop and then burst,

It was—My life is only now beginning,
Until today I dreamed! 1360

SCENE 6

A servant enters, Salome follows.

SALOME *(to the servant).* Were you commanded
To let no person enter unannounced?
I take the blame!
JOSEPH. Salome, you?
SALOME. Who else?
No evil spirit, only your poor wife,
Whom you once wooed as Jacob wooed his Rachel
And whom you now—*(to Mariamne)* Accursed woman, was 1365
It not enough to turn my brother's heart
Away from me? Do you now have to steal
My husband from me too? Both day and night
He thinks of you, as if you were a widow,
And I still less than that! By day he dogs 1370
Your footsteps everywhere! By night he dreams
Of you, and anxiously calls out your name,
He starts up out of sleep—*(to Joseph)* Did I not charge you
With that this very morning? Even today
When all Jerusalem is in revolt, 1375
Today he's not with me, nor in the market
Where I had sent because he did not come,
He is with you, and you—you are alone!
MARIAMNE. It surely is not she. So it is he!
If any doubt were still remaining, then 1380
This silly jealousy has stifled it!—
For him I was a thing and nothing more!
JOSEPH *(to Salome).*
I swear—
SALOME. That I am blind? Oh no! I see!
MARIAMNE. The dying man who would cut down his fig tree
Because he could not bear to have another 1385
Enjoy its fruit when he himself was dead,
He would be culpable, and yet perhaps
He had set out the tree himself and knew
That it would give refreshment to the thief
Or even to the murderer who shook it. 1390
In my case that's not so! And yet! And yet!
That is a crime whose like there never was.
SALOME *(still speaking to Joseph).*
You speak in vain! Commission! What commission?
MARIAMNE. Commission! That the seal!—If it could be,
Then now's the time it would be possible! 1395
But it's not possible! However great

    The turmoil in my breast, my soul is still
    Unsullied by a single base emotion!
    This moment I would give to Antony
    The selfsame answer that I would have given   1400
    Him on our wedding day, I feel that, so it
    Affects me as it does. Were that not so,
    Then I would have to bear it, yes, forgive it!
SALOME *(to Mariamne).*
    You do not seem to see me here!
MARIAMNE.   I do!
    And what is more, you have done me a favor,   1405
    The greatest favor, I was blind and now
    I see, see clearly, and alone through you!
SALOME. You scoff at me? You shall do penance for it,
    If only Herod will return! I will
    Tell everything to him—   1410
MARIAMNE.   What? Oh yes! Do that!
    If he gives ear — — Why not? Why do I laugh?
    Is that impossible? — — And if he listens,
    You have my word, I will not contradict you!
    I do not love myself enough for that!

SCENE 7

ALEXANDRA *(rushes in).* The King!   1415
JOSEPH.   In town?
ALEXANDRA.   Already in the castle!

ACT III

Castle Zion. Alexandra's rooms.

SCENE 1

*Alexandra. Joseph. Salome.
Herod enters with his retinue. Soemus.*

HEROD. Well, here I am! *(to Soemus)* Is it still bleeding? The stone
  Was meant for me, and you were only struck
  Because you came just then to tell me something.
  And so this time your head was your king's shield!
  If you had only stayed back where you were— 1420
SOEMUS. I would not have the wound, nor credit either,
  If credit be deserved. In Galilee
  That man at most is stoned who dares oppose
  Both you and me, for I am but your shadow,
  Or better still your mouthpiece or whatever 1425
  You will.
HEROD.   Yes they are very loyal there,
  At least to their own interests, and to mine
  Because their own go hand in hand with mine.
SOEMUS. How much they do is shown you by the fact
  That you have found me in your capital. 1430
HEROD. In fact, I was surprised to find you here;
  For when the king is gone, there is more need
  Of watchers in the restive provinces!
  What was it then that drove you from your post?
  It certainly can not have been the wish 1435
  To prove to me it was not dangerous
  To leave it, nor was it the premonition
  That there would be a stone to intercept!
SOEMUS. I came to town in all due haste to see
  The Viceroy and disclose direct to him 1440
  A few peculiar facts I have discovered.
  I wanted to report to him, that even
  In Galilee the Pharisees are trying,
  Without success, to undermine the ground;
  And yet my warning came too late, I found 1445
  Jerusalem in flames and I could only
  Help him to put them out!
HEROD *(shakes hands with him).* And that you did
  With your own blood!—Ah, Joseph, greetings to you!
  I thought to find you elsewhere!—Never mind!
  But go at once and bring me Sameas, 1450
  The Pharisee, whom the Roman Captain Titus
  Is holding captive as the Scythians do.
  The stubborn Roman has been hauling him

  Around with him behind the horse he rides,
  Tied to its tail; in his fanatic zeal   1455
  He spit at him upon the open square.
  And so he has to run, as he perhaps
  Has never run before, to keep from falling
  And being dragged along. I should at once
  Have turned him loose as I was riding by!   1460
  My thanks are surely due to him alone
  That now I know who all the serpents are
  Who hitherto have crawled away unseen!
  I now can crush them easily at will! *(exit Joseph)*
HEROD *(to Alexandra)*. I greet you too! And from Mark Antony 1465
  I bring a message to you that you can
  Not hale a river into court, much less
  A king within whose land the river flows,
  Because he did not fill it up with earth!
  (to Soemus) I would have been here long ago, but friends 1470
  Who do not often see each other, find it hard
  To bring themselves to part! And it will be
  That way with us, I tell you in advance,
  Now that I have you here again at last.
  You must be here to help me feast on figs   1475
  As I helped Antony consume the morays,
  Delicious smothered in Falernian wine,
  A gourmand's dish! He had me tell him tales
  About our younger days just to refresh
  His memory! So you must be prepared   1480
  To do the same for me. Though I have not
  So much of the triumphant victor in me,
  That I would ever summon you to me
  As he had summoned me to him, pretending
  That he believed such an absurd complaint,   1485
  With knitted brows like Caesar, armed as well
  With lightning and with thunderbolt
  To make quite sure that I should really come—
  That was the only reason why he did it—
  Yet I shall take advantage of the chance   1490
  Which brings you to Jerusalem today
  And say, as he, when you begin to talk
  About your duty: If you do it, as
  You should, it will not need you every moment!
  You come so rarely that it seems you do   1495
  Not like to come!
SOEMUS.   You do me wrong, and yet
  I have good reason not to come too often!
HEROD *(to Salome)*. Are you here too? So have you learned at last,
  When you meet Mariamne, to imagine
  That you are only looking in a mirror   1500

ACT III, SCENE 1

    And what you see there is your own reflection?
    I often gave that good advice to you
    When you were piqued at her,—you never took it!
    Now do not take the joke amiss and spoil
    The joy of our reunion! But, where is she?   1505
    They told me I would find her with her mother,
    So I came here!
SALOME.   She went when she was told
    That you were coming!
HEROD.   Went? Impossible?
    And yet, perhaps! Since it would be more fitting
    To meet alone!—*(aside)* Do you feel anger, heart,   1510
    Instead of asking pardon?—She is right,
    I'll follow her!
SALOME.   That's right, deceive yourself,
    Explain her fear at seeing you alive,
    Her shame for having thought you dead, and more
    Because she knows she is no longer widow,   1515
    Explain it all as but a maiden's shyness,
    A maiden who has never known a man,
    Not the confusion of a sinful woman!
    She left because of fear!—
HEROD.   Of fear?—Look round you,
    We are not here alone!
SALOME.   That suits me well,   1520
    If I accuse when witnesses are present,
    Then my complaint will be more surely heard,
    And will be harder to suppress!
HEROD.   You place
    Yourself between my wife and me? Take care,
    You might be crushed!
SALOME.   This time I shall not be,   1525
    Although I know how much a sister counts
    With you, when it involves this Maccabee,
    This time—
HEROD.   I have one thing to say! The day
    On which I saw her first, if on that day
    Someone had entered a complaint against her   1530
    He would not easily have found a hearing,
    But easier still than now! Be warned by that!
    I owe so much to her that she can not
    Owe anything to me! I feel it deeply!
SALOME. She has full freedom then?   1535
HEROD.   To wear what mask
    She will to aid her in deceiving you,
    If she finds joy in making sport of you.
SALOME. Then—then I must keep still. Words would be vain!
    Whatever I might say to you, you always

Would have your answer ready: Mummery! 1540
This mummery has had a fair success,
It fooled not me alone, it has deceived
The world as well and it costs you your honor
And me my peace of mind, though you may swear
That Joseph only did what was his duty 1545
When he—but see if any man believes you!

HEROD. When he—what is it you withhold? Go on!
But no — — not yet! *(to a servant)* A message for the Queen.
I ask her presence here!—Does it not seem
As if the whole wide world were free of spiders 1550
And all of them were nesting in my house,
And when for once the blue of heaven seems
To shine for me they start to spin their webs
And hide it as with clouds? In fact—it's strange
She does not come. She really should have kissed me, 1555
Succumbing to the impulse of the moment,
And then have bit her lips in her distress
If after all the ghost had not yet gone!
(to Salome)
You know what you have ventured? Woman, you know?
I was so happy! Understand? And now— 1560
The earth once spilled a glass of wine for me
When I was thirsty, for it started quaking
When I had not yet finished drinking it;
That I forgave because I had to. But now—
On you I could take vengeance!

SCENE 2

Mariamne enters.

HEROD.   Cast yourself 1565
Down at the feet of her you openly
Insulted, then I will not!
SALOME.   Ha!
ALEXANDRA *(aside)*.   That means?
HEROD. Well, Mariamne?
MARIAMNE.   What does the King command?
I have been summoned and I have appeared.
ALEXANDRA *(aside)*. Is this the wife who swore to kill herself, 1570
If he did not return?
HEROD.   Is this your greeting?
MARIAMNE. The King has sent for me to give him greeting,
I give him greeting! Thus the task is done!
ALEXANDRA. How wrong! You stand arraigned before a court.
HEROD. There was a charge about to be preferred 1575
Against you! So I sent for you to come
Before I heard it, but it truly was not

ACT III, SCENE 2

  So that you might defend yourself against it,
  Only because I think it will be stifled
  Quite of itself if you are present here!   1580
MARIAMNE. To hinder that I ought to go again!
HEROD. But Mariamne? Never were you one
  Of those so wretched pitiable souls
  Who, even as they see the face or back
  Of foe, forgive and are once more disgruntled   1585
  Because they are too weak for honest hate,
  Too small to be completely generous.
  What then has so transformed your very soul
  That now you seem to be as one of them?
  Before I left, you gave me a farewell.   1590
  This led me to expect a welcome from you,
  Do you refuse me that? You stand there now
  As if the hills and plains that lay so long
  Between us still were separating us?
  And you step back when I come closer to you?   1595
  Is my return so hateful to you then?
MARIAMNE. Why should it be? It gives me back my life!
HEROD. Gives back your life! Ah! What a word that is!
MARIAMNE. But you will not deny you understand me!
HEROD *(aside)*.
  Can she then know it? *(to Mariamne)* Come!
      (since Mariamne makes no move) Leave us alone! 1600
  (to Alexandra) Pardon!
ALEXANDRA.   Of course!
      (exit; all the others follow her)
MARIAMNE.   The coward!
HEROD.   Coward?
MARIAMNE.   And—
  What shall I call it?
HEROD.   And?—*(aside)* That would be dreadful!
  For never could I blot it out in her!
MARIAMNE. Whether his wife shall follow him in death
  By her own choice, or hangman strike her down—   1605
  It matters not if she but dies! He leaves
  No time for her to sacrifice herself!
HEROD. She knows!
MARIAMNE.   Is Antony a man, as I
  Believed till now, a man like you, or is he
  A daemon as you must believe, since you   1610
  Do seem to doubt there is a sense of duty
  Or remnant of a pride within my bosom
  That would resist, if dripping with your blood
  He came as suitor for my hand and urged me
  To help him while away such leisure time   1615
  As the Egyptian may perchance leave free?

HEROD *(aside).*
  But how? But how?
MARIAMNE.   He would of course have had to
  Put you to death before he could woo me,
  And if you feel yourself so valueless,
  I never would have thought it but I see it,   1620
  That you are fearful, lest the very fullness
  Of manly worth in you would not outweigh him
  In your wife's heart, yet by what right do you
  Believe I am so low, that you should fear
  That I would not repulse the murderer?   1625
  Oh double shame!
HEROD *(breaking out).* What was the price you paid
  To get this secret? For it was not cheap!
  A head was my security!
MARIAMNE.   Salome,
  How well you knew your brother!—Ask the man
  From whom I learned of it what he received,   1630
  No further answer will you get from me! *(turns away)*
HEROD. I'll show you now just how I question him!
  Soemus!

SCENE 3

Soemus enters.

HEROD.   Is my brother Joseph there?
SOEMUS. He waits with Sameas.
HEROD.   Take him away!
  I gave a note to him. Tell him he shall   1635
  Deliver it at once! Accompany him
  And see that everything that it commands
  Is faithfully performed!
SOEMUS.   It shall be done! *(exit)*
HEROD. Whatever you suspect, or think, or know,
  You still misjudge me!   1640
MARIAMNE.   On my brother's murder
  You put the seal of real necessity
  And one must bow to that, however much
  One shudders, but you never will succeed
  In stamping any plan to murder me
  With this same seal, it will remain just what   1645
  It is, a crime one can at most repeat
  But neither now nor ever can surpass!
HEROD. I would not have the courage to reply
  If I, however much I might have risked,
  Had not been sure of what the end would be.   1650
  But sure I was, and I was only sure
  Because I staked my all upon the play!
  I did that which the soldier well may do

ACT III, SCENE 3

In battle sometimes as a last resort,
He hurls the standard from him which he carries,   1655
Upon which fortune, honor, both depend,
Right in the midst of milling foe he hurls it,
But not because he thinks to let it go:
He plunges after it, he brings it back
And brings the laurel too, though sadly torn,   1660
The wreath of victory which even courage
No longer could attain but only desperation.
You called me coward. If a man is that
Who feels a demon in himself and fears it,
Then sometimes I am cowardly, but only   1665
When I must reach my goal by devious paths,
When circumstances force me to pretend
That I am not the man I really am.
Then I am fearful I might show myself
Too soon, and so to tame my pride,   1670
Which easily aroused might spur me on,
I fix on something which is more than I,
On something which must stand or fall with me.
You know what stood before me when I left?
No duel and still less a court of justice,   1675
But a capricious tyrant, in whose presence
I was supposed to hold myself in check
But surely would not if—I thought of you,
And did not even grind my teeth—however
He might offend the man and king in me   1680
While dragging me from feast to feast, and yet
So strangely silent, putting off the pardon;
As patient as a slave I bore it all!

MARIAMNE. You speak in vain! In me you have offended
  Humanity; all who like me are human   1685
  Must share my pain. One need not be my kin,
  One does not need to be like me a woman.
  When you by secret underhanded murder
  Did rob me of my brother, only those
  With brothers could weep with me. All the others   1690
  Could stand aloof, refusing sympathy,
  Dry-eyed. But everyone who breathes has life,
  And no one willingly lets life be taken
  From him save by the hand of God alone,
  Who gave it to him! Such a monstrous crime   1695
  The whole wide human race condemns and hates,
  The fates condemn, who, though they let it start,
  Can not permit completion, you yourself condemn it!
  And if you have so deeply hurt what's human
  In me, then tell me, how is the wife to feel,   1700
  How do I stand with you and you with me?

SCENE 4

Salome rushes in.

SALOME. What awful deed have you in mind? I see
    My husband led away—and he implores me
    To plead with you for mercy—I hesitate,
    For I am angry, do not understand him—   1705
    And now—now fearful whispers reach my ears,
    They say—Their words are lies?
HEROD.   Your husband dies!
SALOME. Before he has been judged? It cannot be!
HEROD. He has been judged and by himself! He had
    The document condemning him to death   1710
    In his own hands before he sinned against me,
    He knew the punishment awaiting him
    If he should do it; he accepted it
    And yet he did it!
SALOME.   Herod, listen to me!
    Are you so sure of that? Oh I complained   1715
    Against him, I believed that I was justified,
    I had good reason for it—that he loved her
    Was obvious, no longer did he have
    A glance for me, or pressure of the hand—
    He was with her by day whenever possible,   1720
    And in the night his dreams betrayed to me
    How much his mind was with her—That is all
    Quite true, and more—And yet it does not follow
    From this, that she must love him in return,
    Still less, I grant, that she—Oh no! oh no!   1725
    My jealousy had carried me too far—
    Forgive! You too forgive. *(to Mariamne)* I hated you!
    Oh God, how fast time flies! They said—Am I
    To love you, as I hated you? Then be
    No longer silent, say that he is guiltless,   1730
    Beg mercy for him, just as I myself!
MARIAMNE. He is!
HEROD.   In her sense, yes—but not in mine!
MARIAMNE. In your sense too!
HEROD.   But then you would not know
    The thing you know! Now nothing can excuse him!
    And if I have him put to death and do   1735
    Not first give him a hearing, then one reason
    I do is this: because I want to show you
    I think no ill of you and deeply rue
    The hasty word I spoke at first in anger,
    But more because I know that he has nothing   1740
    He can say to me!

SCENE 5

SOEMUS *(enters)*.   The bloody work
  Is done! But all Jerusalem's astounded
  And asks just why the very man whom you
  Selected to be Viceroy in your absence,
  When you left here for Egypt, had to lose   1745
  His head at once when you return!
SALOME *(totters)*.   Alas!
        (Mariamne starts to catch her)
  Away! Away! *(to Herod)* And she?
HEROD.   Believe me, sister!
  Your husband has deceived me terribly—
SALOME.   And she?
HEROD.   Not in the way you think—
SALOME.   Then how?
  You want to save your wife. But if my husband   1750
  So terribly deceived you, she did too,
  For what I said is true, and everyone
  Shall know of it who does not know it yet!
  You must now wash in her blood, as in his,
  Else you will ne'er be clean again! You must!   1755
HEROD.   By all that is most sacred to me—
SALOME.   Name
  His crime to me, if that is not the one!
HEROD.   Were I to name it, I should make it greater!
  There was a secret I entrusted to him,
  To me it was important, he betrayed   1760
  This secret, and shall I betray it too?
SALOME.   Wretched excuse, supposed to frighten me!
  You think you can deceive me? You believe
  In everything I told you, but you are
  Too weak to stifle and suppress your love,   1765
  And you prefer to cover the disgrace
  You are unwilling to wipe out. Unless
  You kill me too, your sister, as you did
  My husband, you will not succeed!
        (to Mariamne) He's dead,
  Now you can swear whate'er you will, he will   1770
  Not contradict you! *(exit)*
HEROD.   Follow her, Soemus,
  And try to calm and soothe her! You know her,
  There was a time when she would listen to you!
SOEMUS.   Those times are long since past! But still I go! *(exit)*
MARIAMNE *(aside)*.   I would not ask for mercy for the man   1775
  Who sought to murder me! And yet I shudder—
  There was not even time enough to do it!

HEROD *(aside)*. It simply had to be. He could have had
   Uriah's place assigned to him in battle!
   But now I grant that I regret my haste!   1780

SCENE 6

MESSENGER *(enters)*. I come from Antony!
HEROD.   I know then too
   What word you bring. I must at once make ready.
   The battle is at hand of which he spoke!
MESSENGER. Octavius already has embarked
   For Africa, and Antony has joined   1785
   With Cleopatra and set out with haste
   To clash with him at once near Actium—
HEROD. And then I, Herod, am to be the third!
   Good! I shall go today! Soemus can
   Replace me here although affairs are bad.   1790
   It's well he came!
MARIAMNE.   He has to go again!
   I thank Thee, God!
HEROD *(watching her)*. Ha!
MESSENGER.   No, great King, no!
   His need is not at Actium, he wants
   The Arabs, who have risen in revolt,
   Held down and not allowed to join the foe!   1795
   That is the service he requires of you.
HEROD. It is his place to name the spot to me
   Where I can be of use!
MARIAMNE.   Once more! That gives him
   Another chance!
HEROD *(as before)*. See how my wife rejoices!
                (to the messenger)
   Tell him—but you already know!—*(aside)* Her brow   1800
   Is smooth, her hands are folded as in prayer—
   Such is her heart!
MESSENGER.   But is there nothing else?
MARIAMNE. Now I shall see: was it a fever only,
   The fever of a passion so aroused
   That it confused him, or his inner self   1805
   Which thus betrayed itself to me so clearly?
   Now I shall see!
HEROD *(to the messenger)*. There's nothing more! *(exit messenger)*
                (to Mariamne) Your face
   Now looks more cheerful! But you must not hope
   Too much! One does not always die in war,
   I have returned from war before, so often!   1810
MARIAMNE *(starts to speak but restrains herself)*.
   No! No!

ACT III, SCENE 6

HEROD.   The battle this time is more fierce
 Than e'er before. All other times the struggle
 Was fought for something in the world, but now
 It's for the world itself. It shall decide
 Who rules the world, is it Mark Antony, 1815
 The profligate and libertine, or is it
 Octavius, whose sole claim to merit is
 That never in his life has he been drunk.
 Great blows will be delivered and received,
 Yet it is possible your wish will not 1820
 Be realized, that death may pass me by.
MARIAMNE. My wish! Of course! My wish! It's well this way!
 Be firm, my heart, do not betray yourself!
 The test is none if he suspects what moves you!
 And if he proves his worth, how great is your 1825
 Reward, how great his too can be! Then let him
 Misjudge you! Test him! Keep the end in mind!
 Think of the crown which you can hand to him
 When he has overcome the demon in him!
HEROD. I thank you! You have now relieved my heart! 1830
 Although quite possibly I have transgressed
 Against humanity in you, yet this
 Is clear, I have not sinned against your love!
 So I no longer beg you by that love
 To make a final sacrifice, however, 1835
 I hope that you fulfill one final duty.
 I hope for that not merely for myself,
 For your own sake I hope for it much more.
 You will not want me after this to see
 You only in a fog; since I have sealed 1840
 The dead man's lips I hope you open yours,
 And in his place explain to me, just how
 It came that he presented you his head;
 Because of your humanity you will,
 Because of your own self-respect you will! 1845
MARIAMNE. To keep my self-respect, I will not do it!
HEROD. So you refuse me what is reasonable?
MARIAMNE. Is reasonable! You think it would be that
 For me to fall upon my knees before you
 And swear: Your servant, Sire, did not come near me! 1850
 And so you can believe,—I have no right
 To confidence although I am your wife—
 Hear this besides, and this! Oh shame! Oh shame!
 No, Herod, no! If curiosity
 Should sometime ask, perhaps! Now I am silent! 1855
HEROD. Yet if your love had been but great enough
 To pardon all that I have done for love,
 I never would have asked the question of you!

    But since I know how small it is, I must
    Repeat the question now, for such assurance
    As is afforded by your love can only
    Be as great as is your love itself,
    And any love that values life more highly
    Than the beloved, seems to me quite worthless!
MARIAMNE. And I am silent still!
HEROD.   Then I declare
    I will not kiss the lips again that are
    Too proud to swear no other man has kissed them,
    Until they do it in humility;
    Yes, if there were a means of wiping out
    All memory of you within my heart,
    If I by simply piercing both my eyes,
    Effacing thus the mirror of your beauty,
    Could by that means efface your image too,
    Then I would pierce them in this very hour.
MARIAMNE. Herod control yourself! I think perhaps
    Right now you hold your fate within your hands,
    Mayhap can even turn it as you will!
    For every man at some time comes the moment
    In which the guider of his star gives him
    The reins to hold, and only this is bad,
    He can not know the moment and it may
    Be any that comes rolling by! I feel
    So sure this very one is yours! So stop!
    As you today mark out your course of life
    You well may have to walk it to the end:
    Will you do that in the wild flush of anger?
HEROD. I am afraid you sense but half the truth,
    The turning point is here but is for you!
    For I, what do I want? Only a means
    With which to frighten evil dreams away!
MARIAMNE. I do not want to understand! I bore
    You children! Think of them!
HEROD.   One who is silent,
    As you are, wakes suspicion that he fears
    To tell the truth but does not want to lie.
MARIAMNE. No further!
HEROD.   Good, no further! So farewell!
    And then when I return, let that not rouse
    Your anger too much!
MARIAMNE.   Herod!
HEROD.   Be quite sure
    I will not try again as now to force
    A greeting from you!
MARIAMNE.   There will be no need
    Of that again! *(to Heaven)* Guide Thou his heart, Oh God!

ACT III, SCENE 6

I had forgiven him my brother's murder,
I was prepared to follow him in death,
I still am, can a mortal then do more?
God, Thou hast done what Thou hast never done,
Rolled back the wheel of time, things stand again   1905
Just as before, oh let his actions this time
Be different, then I will forget the past,
Forget it as I would if he had made
A thrust at me in fever with his sword
And then, recovered, bound my wound himself.   1910
(to Herod) Shall I see you again?
HEROD.   If you should see me,
    Then call for chains! For that will prove to you
    That I have gone insane!
MARIAMNE.   You will regret
    This word!—Restrain yourself, oh heart!—You will! *(exit)*
HEROD. It's true, I went too far. Already I   1915
    Have said that to myself. But no less true,
    That if she loved me she would pardon it!
    Yes, if she loved me! Did she ever love me?
    I think she did. But now—Her brother is
    Revenged, though he is dead and in the grave!   1920
    I had him killed to make my crown secure.
    He took with him what matters more: her heart!
    For since her brother died, her attitude
    Toward me is strangely changed. When I compared
    Her with her mother, never did I find   1925
    The slightest trace of similarity,
    Today she seemed in more than one way like her;
    No longer can I trust her as I did!
    That is quite sure! But is it necessary
    That I assume at once she has deceived me?   1930
    The guarantee I had because she loved me,
    That now is gone, a second guarantee
    I still have in her pride, and will a pride
    Which scornfully disdains all self-defense
    Not scorn still more thus to besmirch itself?   1935
    It's true, she knows it! Joseph! Oh! Why can
    Man kill and not awake the dead again?
    He should be able to do both or neither!
    He is revenged! He is not here! And yet
    I see him! "You command?"—It can not be!   1940
    No! I will not believe it! You, Salome,
    Silence! Howe'er it came, it was not thus!
    Perhaps the secret, like a fire inside him,
    Ate through him by itself. Or he betrayed it,
    Because he thought me lost and now he wanted   1945
    To reconcile himself with Alexandra

Before the news arrived here. We shall see!
For I must test her! If I had but dreamed
She ever could find out, I never would
Have gone so far. But since she knows it now,　　　1950
I must go further! For because she knows it,
I now must fear from her revenge those things
Which I had feared from her inconstancy,
Perhaps quite wrongly. I must fear that she
Will celebrate a wedding on my grave!　　　1955
Soemus came quite opportunely. He is
One who would stand where I now stand, were I
Not in the world. His very coming proves
How loyally and zealously he serves me.
I will give him the order now! I know　　　1960
She will lure nothing out of him, if she
Tempts him by human means!—If he betrays me,
She will have paid a price, which is—Salome
Then you were right!—The test will give the answer! *(exit)*

ACT IV

Zion Castle. Mariamne's rooms.

SCENE 1

Mariamne and Alexandra.

ALEXANDRA. Your words and acts are riddles. First your oath: 1965
   If he does not return, I too shall die!
   Then bitter coldness when he came, defiance
   Which could not but arouse his anger, as it
   Gladdened me! Now again the deepest mourning!
   Is there a person who can understand you? 1970
MARIAMNE. If you find that so hard, why vex yourself?
ALEXANDRA. And then the harsh and yet reluctant way
   In which you keep Soemus at a distance!
   One sees that he has something on his mind—
MARIAMNE. You think so? 1975
ALEXANDRA.   Yes! And he would like to tell us,
   Only he does not dare, he would perhaps
   Be doubtful, if he saw you throw yourself
   Into the Jordan, whether he should try
   To rescue you from death; he would be right,
   For you have treated him disdainfully! 1980
MARIAMNE. That is quite true, and Herod can not say,
   .That I have tempted his good friend, that I
   Have lured his secret from him, if he has one,
   By cunning flattery. It's in the hands
   Of Heaven, whether I shall ever learn it! 1985
   I feel it in my heart, I'm risking nothing!

SCENE 2

SAMEAS *(enters, his hands in chains).*
   The Lord is great!
MARIAMNE.   He is!
ALEXANDRA.   You free and yet
   In chains? Another riddle!
SAMEAS.   I will not
   Remove these chains again! Jerusalem
   Shall be reminded by them day by day 1990
   That Jonah's grandson had to sit in prison.
ALEXANDRA. How then did you escape? You bribed the guards?
SAMEAS. I bribed? The guards?
ALEXANDRA.   Of course and yet with what?
   You still have on your woven gown of hair,
   I doubt if they would let you out if you 1995
   Had told them where to find a nest of bees,
   As you well could who know just where to find

　　　　Each hollow tree, for honey is not scarce!
SAMEAS. Why do you ask? Soemus opened up
　　　　The gates for me himself!   2000
MARIAMNE.　　　　　　　　Would he have dared?
SAMEAS. Why not? I thought that you had ordered it.
MARIAMNE. I?
SAMEAS.　　　　No? And yet it seems to me he said so!
　　　　I can be wrong, for I was just repeating
　　　　The last Psalm backwards when he came, and so
　　　　I listened to him with but half an ear!   2005
　　　　Oh well! So then it was the Lord, and I
　　　　Must go up to the Temple to give thanks
　　　　And have no errand here in David's palace!
MARIAMNE. The Lord!
SAMEAS.　　　　　　　The Lord! Was I then justly jailed?
MARIAMNE. Those times are long since past in which the Lord   2010
　　　　Was wont to speak directly to his people.
　　　　We have the law instead, and it speaks for Him!
　　　　The pillar of fire and smoke has ceased to be,
　　　　By which he marked the paths across the deserts
　　　　For our forefathers, and the prophets are   2015
　　　　As silent as the Lord!
ALEXANDRA.　　　　　　　Not all are silent!
　　　　Just recently one prophesied a fire;
　　　　This prophecy was afterward fulfilled!
MARIAMNE. Of course, but he himself had set the fire
　　　　At midnight.   2020
SAMEAS.　　　　Woman! That is blasphemy!
MARIAMNE. It is no blasphemy, I know it happened!
　　　　He is a Pharisee as you yourself,
　　　　He speaks like you, he raves like you, the fire
　　　　Was planned to be the proof he really was
　　　　A prophet able to foresee the future,   2025
　　　　But then a soldier caught him in the act.
SAMEAS. A Roman?
MARIAMNE.　　　　Yes!
SAMEAS.　　　　　　　He lied! He was perhaps
　　　　A hireling! Had perhaps been hired by Herod
　　　　Or hired by you!
MARIAMNE.　　　　Do not forget yourself!
SAMEAS. You are his wife, the wife of the blasphemer   2030
　　　　Who looks upon himself as the Messiah;
　　　　Since you can clasp him in your arms and kiss him,
　　　　You might do other things for him as well!
ALEXANDRA. He looks upon himself as the Messiah?
SAMEAS. He does, he told it to me to my face   2035
　　　　When he was having me led off to prison.
　　　　I cried unto the Lord, I cried: Oh guard

ACT IV, SCENE 3

    Thy people, send us the Messiah whom
    Thou promised us in times of direst need,
    Those times are now upon us! Then he said   2040
    With haughty scorn: Oh He is long since here,
    You merely do not know it! I am He!
ALEXANDRA. Well, Mariamne?
SAMEAS.   With accursed wit
    He proved we are a folk of lunatics
    And he alone enjoys the gift of reason,   2045
    We do not dwell in vain beside the Dead Sea,
    In which there is no ebb and flow of tide,
    And that explains why everyone is tainted.
    It is a faithful mirror of ourselves!
    But he intends to give us life and vigor,   2050
    Even if he must take that stupid book
    Of Moses from us—such his impious words—
    For that bears all the blame that we are not
    More like the Jordan, our clear river, rippling
    Along so merrily, but like a swamp.   2055
ALEXANDRA. He threw away his mask completely?
SAMEAS.   Yes!
    Perhaps, however, when he did, already
    He thought of me as dead; right afterward
    He ordered that I die.
MARIAMNE.   He was provoked!
    He found rebellion here!   2060
SAMEAS.   I now remind you
    Of what your duty is. You must renounce him
    Even as he renounced the Lord! You can
    Thus punish him, for Herod loves you much!
    And when Soemus set me free I thought
    You had already done it. Unless you do it,   2065
    Then do not call the lightning from the clouds
    At all unjust, if it strikes you like him!
    I go to offer sacrifice!
ALEXANDRA.   Then take
    The victim from my flock!
SAMEAS.   I take it where
    It's missed! The widow's lamb, the poor man's sheep!   2070
    What use has God for yours! *(exit)*

SCENE 3

SOEMUS *(comes)*.   Your pardon!
MARIAMNE.   I was
    About to summon you! I bid you welcome!
SOEMUS. This is the first time, is it not?
MARIAMNE.   It is!

SOEMUS. You have avoided me till now!
MARIAMNE.   Have you
    Sought me and have you something then to seek?   2075
    I do not like to think of it.
SOEMUS.   One thing at least:
    Consider me as your most faithful servant!
MARIAMNE. I did, but I no longer do!
SOEMUS.   No longer?
MARIAMNE. How can you open up the prison doors
    And let the rebel out whom Herod jailed?   2080
    Is Herod still the King, or is he not?
SOEMUS. The answer's not as easy as you think!
MARIAMNE. If it is hard, then you will have to suffer!
SOEMUS. You have not heard the battle has been lost!
MARIAMNE. At Actium? The battle has been lost?   2085
SOEMUS. Mark Antony has died by his own hand!
    Queen Cleopatra too, by hers!
MARIAMNE.   She had
    The courage? She could never bear to look
    Upon a sword, recoiled from his when once
    He held it up before her as a mirror!   2090
SOEMUS. It was reported so to Captain Titus!
    Octavius cursed aloud because they were
    Not hindered! I myself read the dispatch!
MARIAMNE. Then Death has had his share for many days
    And every head is safer than it was   2095
    Before!
SOEMUS.   Do you think so?
MARIAMNE.   You smile so strangely!
SOEMUS. It seems you do not know Octavius!
    He will not ask if Death is surfeited,
    He will prepare another feast for him
    Of friends of Antony, there is no lack   2100
    Of dainty morsels for this feast of death!
MARIAMNE. Does that apply to Herod?
SOEMUS.   If he does
    What he proposed—
MARIAMNE.   And what was that?
SOEMUS   He said:
    My love for Antony is past, I would
    Much rather say I hate him, but I shall   2105
    Continue to stand by him till the last,
    Although I am afraid that he must fall,
    I owe it to myself, if not to him!
MARIAMNE. Quite like a king!
SOEMUS.   Yes, like a king! Only
    Octavius is not one to admire it,   2110
    If Herod should do that—

ACT IV, SCENE 3

MARIAMNE. Who dares to doubt?
SOEMUS. Then he is lost indeed, or else they wronged
    Octavius grievously when they held him
    Responsible for all the bloody slaughter
    That followed Caesar's death!   2115
MARIAMNE. That you believe
    So firmly in this outcome, that already
    You number Herod with the dead, is clear,
    Or else you would not dare what you have dared.
    I shudder too, and I admit it freely,
    At your assurance, for you are no fool,   2120
    And surely not without good reason risk
    So much. And yet, however things may stand,
    I still am here and I assure you, that I
    Will find a way to bring obedience
    To him in death, not even one command   2125
    That he has given shall be unfulfilled,
    And that shall be his sacrifice!
SOEMUS. Not one!
    I doubt it, Queen!—*(to himself)* Now let the blow descend!
MARIAMNE. As surely as I am a Maccabee,
    You shall send Sameas back to his prison!   2130
SOEMUS. If you desire it, then it shall be done,
    If you want more, if he shall die, just as
    The King decreed, speak and he is dead!
    But now may I have leave to ask a question:
    Am I, so that the sacrifice you plan   2135
    To offer for the dead may be complete,
    Am I to take my sword and thrust it through you?
    That too is a command he left with me!
MARIAMNE. Alas!
ALEXANDRA. Oh no!
MARIAMNE. So then the end is here!
    And what an end! So dwarfing the beginning   2140
    And everything besides! The past, the future
    As well, for me it all dissolves to nothing.
    I had nothing, I have nothing, I shall
    Have nothing. No one ever was so poor!
ALEXANDRA. Whatever evil deeds you might report   2145
    Of Herod, I could well believe them all,
    But this—
MARIAMNE. Oh do not doubt! For it is true!
ALEXANDRA. Do you say that?
MARIAMNE. Oh God, I know well why!
ALEXANDRA. Then you will know what you must do!
MARIAMNE. Yes, this!
    (she aims the dagger at herself)
ALEXANDRA *(preventing her)*.

Have you gone mad? Is that what he deserves? 2150
That you should act the hangman on yourself?
MARIAMNE. That was reversing it! Thank you! He chose
This office for himself!
     (she hurls the dagger from her)
      Away, you tempter!
ALEXANDRA. You will now seek protection of the Romans!
MARIAMNE. I shall not hinder anyone for whom 2155
That seems important—I myself tonight
Will give a feast!
ALEXANDRA.   A feast!
MARIAMNE.   There I will dance! —
Yes, yes, that is the way!
ALEXANDRA.   And to what end?
MARIAMNE. Ho, servants! *(servants come)*
      Open up the banquet halls!
Invite all those who feel in festive mood! 2160
Light all the candles, any that will burn,
Pluck all the flowers that are not yet wilted!
There is no need of leaving any over!
(to Moses) You once arranged the wedding feast for us,
This feast today must far surpass that other, 2165
So spare no effort! *(she steps forward)* Herod, tremble now!
And even if you never did before!
SOEMUS *(steps up to her).*
I feel the pain as much as you!
MARIAMNE.   I do
Not want your pity! You are not a hangman,
I have no call to doubt, for you have shown it; 2170
Instead you are a traitor, and I can not
Owe thanks to traitors nor endure them round me,
However useful in this world they are.
For this I judge aright! If you had been
The man you seemed to be, God would have had 2175
To work a miracle, He would have had
To give the very air the tongue it lacks;
That He foresaw when He created you,
So He made you the foremost of dissemblers!
SOEMUS. No! That I am not! I was Herod's friend, 2180
I was his brother-in-arms and his companion
Before the throne was his, I was his servant,
Most faithful servant, after he was king.
But only while in me he recognized
The human being, honored him in me, 2185
As I in him the hero and the king.
And that he did, until, unworthily
Dissembling, he cast down his eyes and gave
The dread command by which he heartlessly

ACT IV, SCENE 3

    Consigned both you and me to certain death,   2190
    Exposed me to the vengeance of your people,
    To Roman anger, and to his own spite,
    As he did you to death at my sword's point.
    I then had proof of what I meant to him!
MARIAMNE. And did you give expression to your horror?   2195
SOEMUS. I did not, for I wanted to protect you!
    So I pretended to accept, dissembled,
    If you prefer, so that he would not give
    The order to another, and kill me;
    A Galilean would have done the deed!   2200
MARIAMNE. Forgive my words! You stand to him as I,
    Like me you are offended in your inmost
    Being, like me degraded to a thing!
    He is a friend, just as he is a husband.
    Come to my feast! *(exit)*   2205
ALEXANDRA. So you were waiting too, biding your time,
    As I!
SOEMUS. My time? What do you mean by that?
ALEXANDRA. I always noted with astonishment
    The way you bowed before this king, who owed
    His high position to the Roman's whim,   2210
    The reveller's drunken ecstacy and not
    To race and birth, as if you had forgotten,
    As he had, that you are his equal; now
    I see your aim, you only planned to make
    Him feel secure!   2215
SOEMUS.   In that, you are mistaken!
    I spoke the truth in all. I do not think
    I am his equal and I never shall!
    I know how many rogues there are who serve him
    With grumbling only for the reason: Herod
    Is not his grandson; I know others only   2220
    Are loyal for the sake of Mariamne;
    But I do not belong to any group
    That rather would obey an infant's sword,
    That is inherited, than hero's sword,
    That is but freshly forged and fire hardened.   2225
    I always looked upon him as superior,
    I was as ready to pick up his shield
    For him, my friend-in-arms, when he might let
    It fall, as ever the scepter for the king!
    The crown, the best of women, never did I   2230
    Begrudge him either, for I felt his worth!
ALEXANDRA. But you too are a man!
SOEMUS.   That I have not
    Forgotten that, is what I now am proving!
    None is so great that he may use me as

          A tool! Whoever asks a service of me
          Which—done or not done as it comes—consigns me
          Disgracefully to certain death, that man
          Frees me from every duty; him I have
          To show, that there exists a middle step
          Between the one for kings and that for slaves
          And that on this stands man!
ALEXANDRA.   It makes no difference
          Just what your reason: it's enough to find
          You on my side!
SOEMUS.   No longer fear a struggle,
          He is as good as dead! Octavius
          Is not an Antony, who lets one hack
          Away his flesh and then forgives it freely,
          Because he so admires the hand that does it!
          He only sees the blows!
ALEXANDRA.   And Titus says . . . ?
SOEMUS. He thinks as I! I freed your Sameas
          Only because I wanted her to call
          Me to account. That was the only way
          I knew to get a hearing with the Queen!
          She knows now what she has to know, and is
          Prepared for it when news of death arrives.
          That was my purpose! What a noble woman!
          Kill her! A pity, even if she wept!
ALEXANDRA. Surely, a tender husband!—Talk to her,
          Persuade her if you can that she should seek
          Protection with the Romans, and yourself
          Come to the feast by which she breaks with Herod,
          Be he now dead or still alive! *(exit)*
SOEMUS *(following her)*.   He's dead!

SCENE 4

          Servants enter and make arrangements for the feast.
MOSES. Well Artaxerxes? Lost again in thought?
          Come, come! You're not the clock with us, you know!
ARTAXERXES. If you had had that job for years, as I have,
          Then your reactions would be quite like mine!
          Especially if every night you dreamed
          You had the former duty to discharge!
          With my right hand I grasp the left hand's pulse
          Involuntarily and count and count
          And often count to sixty beats, before I
          Remember I no longer am a clock!
MOSES. Remember then that here with us your job
          Is not to measure time! For that we have
          The sundial and the sand! And you have things

ACT IV, SCENE 4

    To do in time, just like the rest of us!   2275
    It's loafing, nothing else!
ARTAXERXES.   I swear it's not!
MOSES. Be still! You never count while you are eating!
    And furthermore, we do not swear here either,
    And *(to himself)* if the King himself were not half Gentile
    We would not have a foreign servant either!   2280
    There the musicians come already! Hurry! *(joins the others)*
JEHU. You, is that really true what people tell
    About you?
ARTAXERXES.   Why then should it not be true?
    Must I confirm the tale a hundred times?
    That at the satrap's court I was the clock   2285
    And was much better off than here with you!
    At night I was relieved, then 'twas my brother,
    And daytimes too, when it was time to eat.
    I do not feel so grateful to your King
    That with the other prisoners of war   2290
    He dragged me here. I grant my work at last
    Was getting hard. I had to go along
    To war, and when you see the arrows flying
    And people falling all around, you are
    More apt to miss the count than in a hall   2295
    Where people come together for a dance.
    I shut my eyes, for I am not a hero
    The way my father was. An arrow hit him
    While at his post—he also was a clock,
    As we, my brother too, and I, we all   2300
    Were clocks—he called the hour and died! How's that?
    That was a man! That took a deal more courage
    Than it required to shoot the arrow at him!
JEHU. Have you no sand at home then? Is that why
    You have to do that?   2305
ARTAXERXES.   We? Have we no sand?
    More than enough to cover all Judea!
    It's only that our satrap, so they say
    Has every thing much better than the others.
    The pulse of man, you know, beats more exactly,
    If he is well and does not have a fever,   2310
    Than ever any sand runs through a tube.
    And of what use to you are sundials then,
    On days it does not suit the sun to shine?
    (counts) One— two—
MOSES *(returns).*   Be off! The guests are coming now!
ARTAXERXES. Is that a feast? I have seen different feasts,   2315
    Where only food was eaten that had come
    From foreign countries! Where a guest was punished,
    Yes even put to death, if he should dare

|To drink a drop of water, and where men
|Who had been wrapped in hemp well soaked with pitch 2320
|Were later set ablaze and burned by night
|As torches in the gardens—
MOSES. Stop! What crime
|Against your satrap had those men committed?
ARTAXERXES. Committed? Nothing! Funerals with us
|Are much more splendid than are weddings here! 2325
MOSES. Presumably you feast upon your dead?
|That would go well with all the rest!
ARTAXERXES. Perhaps
|It is not true then either that your Queen
|Dissolved a pearl once in a glass of wine,
|A pearl more valuable than all the kingdom, 2330
|And that she gave a beggar this same wine,
|Who drank it as he would have any other!
MOSES. That is not true, thank God!
ARTAXERXES *(to Jehu).* You said it was!
JEHU. Because it seemed to me to be an honor for her
|And I had heard it told of the Egyptian! 2335
MOSES. Get out!
ARTAXERXES *(points to the roses Jehu carries).*
|Are those real roses? They are cheap,
|With us all roses are of gold and silver!
|They ought to send them where the flowers are
|As valuable as gold and silver here!
The servants scatter. The guests, Soemus among them, have been gathering during the last half of this scene. Music. Dancing. Silo and Judas leave the others and step forward.
SILO. What is the reason for this feast? 2340
JUDAS. The reason?
|The King is coming back! And that today!
SILO. Really?
JUDAS. How can you ask! What other reason
|Could there well be for such a festival?
|Best practice some new way to bow and scrape!
SILO. Did they not say— 2345
JUDAS. All lies! It always is
|When rumor says some ill has come to him!
|And that is natural, there are so many
|Who wish him ill! Besides, do people dance
|In homes where they are mourning for the dead?
SILO. Then very soon the blood will flow in streams, 2350
|The jails are full to bursting since the riot!
JUDAS. I know that better far than you can know it,
|I dragged so many into jail myself.
|This riot was so absolutely senseless
|That everyone was forced to fight against it 2355

ACT IV, SCENE 5

    Who did not crave a hanging for himself.
    You know I have no love at all for Herod,
    However deeply I may bow before him,
    But what he says is right: the Romans are
    Too powerful for us, we are no more   2360
    Than insects are within the lion's jaws,
    They dare not sting, for they would be devoured!
SILO. I'm only sorry for my gardener's son
    Who threw a stone right at a Roman eagle
    And hit it too! That is hard luck for him.   2365
JUDAS. How old is he?
SILO.   How long ago was it
    I broke my ankle?—That's when he was born,
    For then his mother could not be my nurse,
    That's right—he's twenty!
JUDAS.   There's no danger then!
    (Mariamne and Alexandra appear)
    The Queen! *(starts to go)*   2370
SILO.   Why not? What do you mean? Explain!
JUDAS. Well then! In confidence! Since he is twenty
    There is no danger, but were he nineteen
    Or twenty-one, it would be bad for him!
    Next year it will be different!
SILO.   Do not joke!
JUDAS. I tell you it is true! You wonder why?   2375
    The King himself is father of a son
    Of twenty years, and yet he does not know him!
    When he deserted her, the mother took
    The child away and swore a solemn oath
    She would corrupt the child—   2380
SILO.   Frightful woman!
    A Gentile?
JUDAS.   Probably! I do not know!—
    But so that he would have to kill his son,
    You understand? I think it was a frenzy
    Which then subsided after her first rage,
    Yet he is anxious, and no decree of death   2385
    Has ever been enforced against a man
    Whose age was that of Herod's son.
    Comfort your gardener! But keep it to yourself!
    (they lose themselves among the others)

SCENE 5

    Alexandra and Mariamne in the foreground.
ALEXANDRA. You will not seek protection of the Romans?
MARIAMNE. Why should I?   2390
ALEXANDRA.   To be sure you stay alive!

MARIAMNE. Alive! Of course! One has to stay alive!
  Pain has no sting unless one is alive!
ALEXANDRA. At least then you should give the hour its due!
  You hold a feast, so you should show your guests
  A festive face, as is but fit and proper!   2395
MARIAMNE. I am no instrument nor yet a candle,
  Am not supposed to sound nor yet to shine,
  So take me as I am! No! Do not do it!
  Urge me to whet the axe for my own neck,
  What am I saying, urge me to make merry—   2400
  Cheer up, Soemus!
        (to Salome as she enters and approaches)
                    You Salome? Welcome
  Especially to me, although in mourning!
  I scarcely hoped for that!

SCENE 6

SALOME.   I have to come
  If I desire to know how matters stand!
  I am invited to attend a feast   2405
  But no one tells me why the feast is held!
  I may suspect, but really I must know!
  You are expecting Herod back? We shall
  See him today? The candles tell me yes,
  The merry music! You must tell me too!   2410
  I do not ask for me! But as you know—
  No, no, you do not know, you have forgotten,
  Perhaps you dreamed that she was dead and buried,
  Else you would not have kept the news from her,
  Only your dream deceived you, for she still   2415
  Is sitting in the corner where she sat
  When she blessed you—
MARIAMNE.   What is it you are saying?
SALOME. Enough! For Herod has a mother still,
  Who pines away with worry for her son.
  And I, I beg you: Do not let her longer   2420
  Do penance for the crime of bearing me,
  Give her the comfort which her heart requires!
MARIAMNE. I have no comfort I can give his mother!
SALOME. Today then you are not expecting Herod?
MARIAMNE. No, not at all! I heard that he was dead!   2425
SALOME. And yet you celebrate?
MARIAMNE.   Since I still live!
  And shall one not rejoice that one still lives?
SALOME. That—I do not believe!
MARIAMNE.   Thanks for your doubt!
SALOME. The candles—

ACT IV, SCENE 7

MARIAMNE. Are intended to shed light.
SALOME. The cymbals— 2430
MARIAMNE. Must resound, why else have cymbals?
SALOME *(points to Mariamne's festive clothing).*
  The jewels—
MARIAMNE. Would of course become you better—
SALOME. That indicates—
MARIAMNE. A joyous festival!
SALOME. But held above a grave—
MARIAMNE. Quite possible!
SALOME. Then—Mariamne, hear a serious word!
  I always hated you, but always I 2435
  Have doubted whether it was justified,
  And penitent I often came to you
  To—
MARIAMNE. Kiss me! Once you even did it too!
SALOME. But now I see that you are—
MARIAMNE. Rude enough
  To leave you standing here alone, and join 2440
  The group beginning dancing over there!
  Soemus!
SOEMUS *(offers his arm).* Yes, my Queen!
MARIAMNE. I am quite sure
  That Herod saw me thus, when he gave you
  The bloody order. Is it not amazing!
  Now everything has come as he expected! 2445
    (as she goes away, to Salome)
  You will look on?
    (with Soemus backstage where they are no longer seen)
SALOME. This woman is still worse
  Than I had thought! And that is saying much!
  That's why she has the brilliant serpent's skin
  With which she lures all men!—Yes, she is dancing!
  Well, truly, now my conscience is at rest, 2450
  No one on earth can do her an injustice!
    (she watches Mariamne)

SCENE 7

Alexandra comes with Titus.

ALEXANDRA. Titus, you notice how my daughter mourns!
TITUS. Perhaps she has some further news from Herod?
ALEXANDRA. The news that all is over with him! Yes!
TITUS *(looks at Mariamne).*
  She dances!
ALEXANDRA. Like a bride, not like a widow! 2455
  Titus, until today she wore a mask,
  And, mark you, she was not the only one!

TITUS. It's for her good! She stays then what she is!
      If she is one of Herod's enemies
      She will not have to suffer with his friends!   2460
ALEXANDRA. To show us that, she gives this festival!
                (turns away from Titus)
TITUS. These women send a thrill of horror through me!
      The one hews off the hero's head, whom she
      Has just won over with her traitorous kisses,
      While he is still asleep, the other dances   2465
      Like mad upon the grave of her dead husband
      Because she wants to keep the crown herself!
      I surely was invited here to see that—
                (he looks at Mariamne again)
      Yes, yes, I see and will report in Rome—
      But here I shall not drink a drop of wine!   2470
SALOME. Well, Titus, what do you say? Is the King
      So badly off that she may venture all?
TITUS. If he did not go over to Octavius
      At once and help to give Mark Antony
      The final blow even before his fall,   2475
      And that I doubt, then things look bad for him!
SALOME. If he had only done it!—If she should keep
      Her head, then I do not know why the Lord
      Gave dogs the flesh of haughty Jezebel
      To eat! *(she mingles with the others)*   2480
TITUS.   She goes on dancing, but it seems
      It is not easy for her! She ought to glow,
      But she is pale, as if in thought she were
      Some other place and only following
      The dance mechanically! Well even Judith   2485
      May well have felt some fear while at her task!
      This woman too must still feel on her lips
      The last kiss of the husband whom she now
      So solemnly renounces here before me,
      And she has not yet seen him dead!—She comes!
Mariamne appears again. Alexandra and Soemus follow her.
ALEXANDRA *(to Mariamne).*
      I spoke with Titus!   2490
MARIAMNE *(as she turns sees her image in the mirror)*
                Ha!
ALEXANDRA.   What is the matter?
MARIAMNE. Just so I saw myself once in my dreams!—
      So it was that, which would not let me rest
      Until I found the ruby I had lost
      Which gleams so somber now upon my breast:
      The picture would not be complete without it!—   2495
      The last scene follows soon!
ALEXANDRA.   Come to yourself!

MARIAMNE. Let me alone!—A mirror quite like that!
  At first a little dimmed as by the breath
  Of someone, then quite gently clearing, like
  The images it showed me one by one, 2500
  And gleaming finally like polished steel.
  I saw my life entire! First I appeared
  A child enveloped in a rosy light
  That slowly changed into a deeper red:
  The features, though my own, seemed strange to me 2505
  And only in the third clear transformation
  I recognized my own too youthful face.
  And now there came the maiden and the moment
  When Herod led me to the flower garden
  And said to me with ardent flattery: 2510
  Of all these flowers none is too beautiful
  For your dear hand to pluck!—Accurst be he
  That he forgot it so completely!—Then it
  Became uncanny and against my will
  I had to see the future. So and so 2515
  I saw myself—and last as I stand here!
  (to Alexandra) Is it not strange, a dream so comes to life?—
  The gleaming mirror now grew dull again,
  The light turned ashen hue and I myself,
  Who had just been so glowing, was as pale 2520
  As if my blood had long been flowing out
  From all my veins beneath this festive garment;
  My flesh did creep, I cried: Now I am coming
  As skeleton and that I will not see!
  I turned away—*(she turns away from the mirror)* 2525
VOICES IN THE BACKGROUND. The King! *(general commotion)*
ALEXANDRA. What? Who?

SCENE 8

Herod enters, in military dress. Joab. Retinue.
MARIAMNE. It's Death! Grim Death! Yes, Death is here
    among us!
  And unannounced, just as he always comes!
SALOME. Yes, death for you! You feel it close upon you!
    My brother!
    (she is about to embrace Herod, he pushes her away)
HEROD. Mariamne! *(he draws near)*
MARIAMNE. Draw your sword!
  Prepare the poison cup! For you are Death! 2530
  And Death's embrace and kiss is sword and poison!
HEROD *(turns to Salome).* What does it mean? Already from afar
  A thousand candles called out through the night:
  Your messenger is safe, he was not captured

      By Arabs, he arrived, you are expected,   2535
      And now—
SALOME.   The candles have deceived you badly,
      They were rejoicing here, they thought you dead!
      Your messenger did not arrive, your mother
      Has rent her garments over you!
          (Herod looks around, sees Titus, and beckons him)
TITUS *(steps forward)*.   It's so!
      Here no man was prepared, not even I,   2540
      To think you would desert Mark Antony
      Before the battle lost at Actium
      And join your force to Caesar's, as good judgment
      So clearly counseled! That this is what you did
      Is proved to me by your return. Well then!   2545
      I—wish you luck!
MARIAMNE *(joins them)*. And I lament the fact
      That opportunity was not presented
      To slay Mark Antony with your own hand.
      Thus you would best have shown to your new lord
      That you no more had interest in the old one;   2550
      You would have brought your friend's head with you for him,
      He would have paid you for it with the crown!
HEROD. Shame, Titus, shame! You too think that of me?
      I marched right down into Arabia
      As Antony had bidden me to do,   2555
      But there I found no enemy! So I
      Set out for Actium and it was not
      My fault that I arrived too late. If he
      Had held, as I believed he would and could,
      I would *(to Mariamne)* have sought the opportunity   2560
      To pay him for the crown by giving him
      Octavius' head! *(to Titus)* But he did not! He was
      Already dead when I appeared, a friend
      Was now no longer necessary, and I
      Sought out Octavius; but not as king—   2565
      I laid the crown aside—I did not go
      As beggar either. I drew my sword and said:
      I planned to use this sword against you, might
      Perhaps have colored it with your own blood
      Had things been different here. But that is over!   2570
      I lower it before you, lay it down!
      Consider now how firm a friend I was,
      Not whose; dead Antony has set me free!
      Henceforth I can be your friend if you will!
TITUS. And he?
HEROD.   He said: where have you left your crown?   2575
      I want to add another jewel to it,
      The province you have lacked! For you shall feel

ACT IV, SCENE 8

    It only in my generosity
    That I am victor, not Mark Antony.
    He never would have taken it away   2580
    From Cleopatra, I present it to you!
TITUS.   That—I should never have believed. I praise
    Your star alone!
HEROD.   Oh Titus, do not praise it!
    For I was spared for onerous tasks! Soemus!
          (Soemus stays where he is and does not answer)
    Did you betray me? You are mute! I know   2585
    Enough! Away with him!
SOEMUS *(while being led away).* I make no plea!
    But you may well believe I thought you dead!
    Now do what pleases you! *(exit)*
HEROD.   And after death
    It all ends, does it not? Yes! Yes! My Titus,
    If you had known the man as I — — You would not   2590
    Be standing here as calm and self-possessed
    As I am, you would gnash your teeth and froth
    With rage and cry in anger: *(to Mariamne)* Woman, what did
    You do to make him go so far?—Salome,
    You were right, I must wash and wash myself—   2595
    I must have blood! The Court shall sit at once!
    (to Mariamne) Still silent? Taking refuge in defiance?
    And I know why! You still remember what
    You were to me! It would be easier
    To tear my heart out of my breast—yes, Titus—   2600
    Than *(again to Mariamne)* you out of my heart. And yet I do it!
MARIAMNE *(turns abruptly).*
    I am a prisoner?
HEROD.   Yes!
MARIAMNE *(to the soldiers).* Take me hence!
    (turns—at a sign from Herod, Joab follows her with soldiers)
    Death can not be my husband any longer! *(exit)*
HEROD. Ha! Ha! Once long ago I said to her:
    Two people can not ever one outlive   2605
    The other, if their love is deep and true,
    And even if I fell on distant fields;
    One would not need to send a messenger,
    For you at once would feel it when it happened,
    Without a wound would die with me of mine!   2610
    Oh Titus, do not laugh at me! It's true!
    But people do not love each other so! *(exit)*

ACT V

Large audience room as in the first act. Throne and judges' table.

SCENE 1

Herod and Salome.

HEROD. Enough! I have directed that the Court
  Shall sit and I shall execute its sentence!
  Yes I, who used to fear each sign of fever, 2615
  And if it only struck her waiting-woman,
  Now I myself am arming death against her!
  It is enough! And if your zeal will still
  Not let you rest, then it will miss its goal
  And I shall surely think that hate alone 2620
  Speaks from your lips, and as a witness shall
  Reject you, even though I let each candle
  Bring evidence, that was ablaze that night,
  And every flower that filled the air with fragrance!
SALOME. But Herod! I will not deny that I 2625
  Have often hunted for her failings and
  Have magnified them, just as you the virtues
  That you discovered in her. Could the pride
  With which she never failed to treat your mother
  And me, could such a pride inspire love? 2630
  She thought herself a higher type of being,
  But one which never did arouse in me
  Another thought than this: What is the need
  Of that thick book in which we are informed
  About the Maccabees' heroic deeds? 2635
  The chronicle is written on her face!
HEROD. Your aim is to refute me, and you seal
  The judgment I pronounced!
SALOME.   Pray hear me out!
  I grant that it was so. But if I now
  Said more than what I know and think and feel, 2640
  Yes, if because of sisterly compassion
  I did not still lock in my breast the half
  Of what I might have said, then may my child—
  I love him dearly!—live as many years
  As there are hairs that grow upon his head, 2645
  And may each day bring him as many pangs
  As it has minutes, yes, as it has seconds!
HEROD. The oath is terrible!
SALOME.   And yet I find
  It easier to say than: Night is black!
  My eye might well be sick, but scarcely could 2650
  It be, that at the same time with the eye

The ear be sick, the heart, the instinct, all
The other organs that support my senses!
And this time all of them are in agreement,
As if they could not contradict each other. 2655
Yes, if upon that festive night the Lord
Had cried out to me from the vault of Heaven:
From what dire evil shall I free your earth,
You have your choice, then I would not have named
The plague, I would have named your wicked wife! 2660
I shuddered at the sight of her, it seemed
As if I had stretched out my human hand
In darkness to a demon out of Hell
And he were scoffing at me for it, stepping
Forth from that stolen body of flesh and blood 2665
And in his own so terrifying form
Were leering at me through the smoke and flames;
Not only I was shuddering so, even
The Roman, hardened Titus, was amazed!
HEROD. Indeed, and he weighs heavier than you, 2670
For as he loves no one, he hates no one,
And he is just, like spirits without blood.
Now leave me, for I am expecting him!
SALOME. No, no, I never shall forget this dance
At which she moved in rhythm with the music 2675
And yet as if she knew for certain you
Lay dead beneath the ground! By God, I would
I did not have to say that! For I know
How it must rouse you, who have sacrificed
Your mother, sister, and much more for her! 2680
But so it was! *(exit)*

SCENE 2

HEROD *(alone).* What Titus told me was
The same! Besides I saw enough myself!
And she is right! I sacrificed my sister
For her, almost my mother: would not they
Outweigh the one, the brother she has lost? 2685
In her eyes they would not!

SCENE 3

Titus enters.
HEROD. Well, Titus, has
Soemus yet confessed?
TITUS. The things you know!
No more!
HEROD. And not—

TITUS.   Oh no! He flared right up
   In rage when I remotely hinted at it!
HEROD. I could expect it!   2690
TITUS.   Never had there lived
   A wife like yours and never had there been
   A man so little worthy of the jewel
   That God had granted him—
HEROD.   As I myself!
   Yes, yes!—"He did not know what pearls were worth,
   Therefore I stole them from him," said the thief.   2695
   I do not think it helped.
TITUS.   Her heart was rarer
   Than gold—
HEROD.   He knows it? He is all aglow,
   Praises the wine! Is that not proof enough
   That he has tasted it? What reason did
   He give you? Why did he betray my order   2700
   To her?
TITUS.   Abhorrence, so he said!
HEROD.   Abhorrence?
   And did not say a word to me about it?
TITUS. Would that have been advisable for him?
   Could you have let the stubborn servant live
   Who ever once received an order from you   2705
   And then refused it?
HEROD.   Was it not enough?
   In such a case, to leave it unfulfilled?
TITUS. Of course! If he went further, then he did it
   Perhaps because you seemed already lost
   And now at your expense he may have wished   2710
   To gain himself the favor of the Queen
   In whose two hands his future fortune lay.
HEROD. No, Titus, no! Soemus was the man
   To risk the stroke himself, that makes the favor
   Of any other quite unnecessary!   2715
   Therefore I gave the charge to him, I thought:
   He certainly will do it for himself,
   If not for you! Were he a lesser man,
   Did he not have so many friends in Rome,
   I might perhaps believe, but now—No, no!   2720
   There was one reason only!
TITUS.   Yet he will not
   Admit that one!
HEROD.   He would not be the man
   He is, if he admitted it. He knows
   Full well what must now follow and he hopes
   By his denial to awake in me   2725
   A final doubt which, if it does not save

ACT V, SCENE 4

His head for him, may yet guard hers from death!
But he is wrong, the doubt lacks any sting,
For had I nothing that she did to punish,
I have what she became and what she is!　　　　2730
Ah! Had she ever been what she appeared:
She never could have so transformed herself;
And I take vengeance on the hypocrite!
Yes, Titus, yes, I swear it by the key
To paradise she holds within her hands;　　　　2735
By all the happiness which she has brought
To me, and all the joy she still could bring;
Yes by the shudder which just now has warned me
That I shall but destroy myself in her:
Yes make an end, however it may be!　　　　2740

TITUS. It is too late to cry a warning to you:
　Oh do not give the order! and I know
　No means myself that can bring clarity
　And so I do not dare to say: Desist!

SCENE 4

Joab enters.

HEROD. Are they convened?　　　　2745
JOAB. 　　　　　　　Long since! And from the prison
　I must report what seems important to me!
　I must report that Sameas can not
　Be brought to kill himself!
HEROD. 　　　　　　　My order was
　That torture be inflicted till he does!
　(to Titus) I heard that he had sworn to kill himself　　　　2750
　If he could not make me the like of him,
　Not break the Gentile streak in me—
　He calls it that. Since he did not succeed
　In that, I force him now to keep his oath,
　He has deserved that death a thousandfold!　　　　2755
TITUS. I would have strongly urged his death myself,
　He has affronted me and Rome in me
　And that can everywhere be freely pardoned
　But not here, where the people are so headstrong!
HEROD *(to Joab).* Well then!　　　　2760
JOAB. 　　　　　　　They did exactly as you ordered,
　Only it did not help at all. The hangman
　Tried almost every torture on him. He gave
　Him wounds besides, for he was angered so
　By his defiance, which he took for scorn,
　But it is just as if he lashed a tree,　　　　2765
　As if he had been cutting into wood:
　The old man stands as if he had felt nothing,

He sings instead of screaming and makes no move
To grasp the dagger which they hold before him,
He sings the psalm the three men sang when they 2770
Were in the burning fiery furnace, sings
More loudly still at each new pang of torture,
And when he stops, he even prophesies!
HEROD (aside). Yes, that is how they are!—Will she be different?
JOAB. As if he had received the gift of eyes 2775
For secret and mysterious things, as many
As he has wounds, he cries aloud: The time
Is now fulfilled and at this sacred moment
The Virgin Mother of the tribe of David
Is laying in the manger bed a Child 2780
Who will cause thrones to topple, wake the dead,
Tear stars from Heaven, and will rule the world
From everlasting, unto everlasting!
The mob meanwhile has gathered there in thousands,
Awaits outside the gates, hears everything, 2785
Believes Elijah will again send down
The chariots of fire to carry him
To Heaven like the prophet. Even a hangman
Was terrified and held the old wounds closed
Instead of wounding him anew! 2790
HEROD. They shall
Put him to death at once; when he is dead,
Shall show him to the people!—And then bid
The judges come as well and—
JOAB. and the Queen! (exit)
HEROD. You, Titus, will please sit beside me here!
I also sent a summons to her mother, 2795
So she shall feel no lack of witnesses.

SCENE 5

Aaron and the other five judges enter. Alexandra and Salome follow.
Joab enters immediately after them.
ALEXANDRA. My King and Lord, I give you greeting!
HEROD. Thank you!
He seats himself upon the throne, Titus sits down beside him, the judges at a sign from him take seats in a semicircle round the table.
ALEXANDRA *(while this is taking place).*
I think of Mariamne's fate as something
Distinct from mine, and save myself, as if
I were a torch, for what is yet to come. 2800
(she sits down beside Salome)
HEROD *(to the judges).*
You know why I have had you summoned here!
AARON. It was with deepest pain that we appeared!

HEROD. I do not doubt that! You are all related
  Or stand on terms of friendship with my house,
  So what hurts me, hurts you! You will be glad   2805
  Then, if the Queen, whom I—*(he hesitates)* But spare me that!
  You will be glad, if you do not condemn her,
  If you may send her home to me, instead
  Of sending her to Golgotha, and yet
  If that necessity arises, you will   2810
  Not lose your courage but will face the worst,
  For as you share my fortune and misfortune
  So you will share disgrace and honor too.
  Proceed then!
  He gives Joab a sign. Joab goes and returns with Mariamne.
        A long pause follows.
HEROD.   Aaron!
AARON.   Queen! Our task is not
  An easy one! You stand before your judges!   2815
MARIAMNE. Before my judges, yes, and also you!
AARON. Do you not recognize this Court?
MARIAMNE.   I see
  A higher one! If that permits an answer
  To questions that you ask, then I shall speak,
  And shall keep silent, if that Court forbids!—   2820
  My eyes can scarcely see you, for behind you
  Stand spirits that regard me, silent, solemn;
  They are the famous forebears of my race.
  For three long nights I saw them in my dreams
  And now they come by day as well, I know   2825
  Exactly what it means to see the dance
  Of death already opened up for me
  And all who live and breathe becoming pale;
  There right behind that throne on which a king
  Appears to sit, stands Judas Maccabaeus: 2830
  Hero of Heroes, gaze not down so darkly
  On me, you shall be satisfied with me!
ALEXANDRA. Not too defiant, Mariamne!
MARIAMNE.   Mother!
  Farewell!—*(to Aaron)* Of what then do I stand accused?
AARON. That you deceived your king and husband—
                          (to Herod) Is   2835
    That right?
MARIAMNE.   Deceived? And how? Impossible!
  Did he not find me as he thought he would?
  Did he not find me dancing and at play?
  Did I put on deep mourning when I heard
  That he was dead? Did I shed tears of grief?   2840
  Or tear my hair? Oh, I would then have been
  Deceiving him, but I did not do that

    And I can prove it. Speak your mind, Salome!
HEROD. I found her as she says. She does not need
  To look around to find another witness.   2845
  But never, never had I thought it of her!
MARIAMNE. Not thought it? Yet you stationed close behind me
  The hangman in his mask? That can not be!
  For as I stood before his mind at parting,
  Just so he found me after his return,   2850
  And so I must deny that I deceived him!
HEROD *(breaking out in wild laughter)*.
  So she did not deceive me, since she only
  Did what foreboding, premonition let
  Me fear—How much I praise that sinister
  Admonisher!—*(to Mariamne)* Ah! Woman! That is like you! 2855
  But do not build too much upon the hope
  That I, with joy and peace, have also lost
  My strength, perhaps enough is left for vengeance
  And—even as a boy I always shot
  An arrow after birds if they escaped me.   2860
MARIAMNE. Speak not of premonition and foreboding
  But speak of fear alone! You quaked at that
  Which you deserved! That is the way of man!
  You can no longer trust the sister, since you
  Have put to death the brother; you have done   2865
  Most frightful things to me and now you think
  I must reply, yes, even must outdo you!
  No? Or did you, when you were facing death
  In honest open warfare, always station
  A hangman right behind me? You are silent?   2870
  It's well. Since you yourself do feel so deeply
  What is most fitting for me, since your fear
  Instructs me what my duty is, so then
  I finally fulfill this sacred duty,
  And separate myself from you forever!   2875
HEROD. Answer! Do you confess? Or do you not?
MARIAMNE *(is silent)*.
HEROD *(to the judges)*.
  You see, there is no frank confession! Also
  I do not have the proof you like to have!
  But once you did condemn a murderer
  To death because one of his victim's jewels   2880
  Was found on him. It was of no avail
  To show his hands, which he had washed so clean,
  Nor yet to swear the dead man's jewel had been
  A gift; you had the sentence carried out!
  It stands the same way here! She has a jewel,   2885
  An evidence, more incontestible
  For me than any human tongue could give,

ACT V, SCENE 5

    That she is guilty of the sin of sins.
    A miracle would not have merely happened,
    It would have had to be repeated, were it   2890
      Not so, and miracles are not repeated!
MARIAMNE *(moves as if to speak)*.
HEROD. Yes, she will say, just as the murderer said:
    It had been given her! And she may risk it,
    For like a forest, bedrooms too are mute.
    But if you should be tempted to believe her   2895
    Then all my inmost feelings contradict you
    And every explanation possible is
    Against you too, and I demand her death.
    In truth, her death! I do not want to drain
    The loathesome cup defiance offers me,   2900
    Nor to torment myself from day to day
    With wondering whether such defiance is
    The most unpleasant face of innocence, or
    The boldest mask of sin, I want to save
    Myself from this mad whirl of love and hate   2905
    Before it stifles me, cost what it may!
    And so away with her!—You hesitate?
    That is my will!—Or do you differ with me?
    Then speak! I know it's time that I were silent!
    So speak then! Do not sit like Solomon   2910
    Between the mothers with the two young babes!
    The case is clear! To judge, you need no more
    Than what you see! A woman, who can stand there
    As she does, merits death and were she free
    From every guilt! And still you do not speak?   2915
    Do you perhaps first want the proof, how firmly
    I am persuaded that she has deceived me?
    I give it to you with Soemus' head,
    And that at once! *(he turns to Joab)*
TITUS *(rises)*.   I don't call this a court!
    Pardon! *(he is about to go)*   2920
MARIAMNE.   No, Roman, stay, I recognize it!
    And who will challenge it, if I do not!
    *(Titus sits down again, Alexandra stands up, Mariamne steps
        up to her, in an undertone)*
    You have brought sorrow to me, never have
    You judged your happiness in terms of mine!
    If I'm to pardon that, keep silence now!
    You will not alter what I have resolved!   2925
        (Alexandra sits down)
    Well, judges?
AARON *(to the rest)*. Any one of you who thinks
    The King's decree unjust, let him arise!
        (all remain sitting)

So you have all decreed that she shall die!
   (he stands up)
You are condemned to death, my Queen!—Have you
Aught else you wish to say?   2930
MARIAMNE.   Unless the hangman
Has had his orders in advance, already
Is waiting for me with the axe, I wish
To speak with Titus yet, before I die.
(to Herod) It is the custom to allow a wish
To one about to die. If you can grant it,   2935
Then let my life be added to your own!
HEROD. The hangman has no orders yet—I can!
And since you promise me eternity
As my reward for that, I must and will!
(to Titus) Is not this woman terrible?   2940
TITUS.   She stands
Before a man, as woman never should!
So make an end of it!
SALOME *(steps forward)*. Oh do! Your mother
Is sick and close to death! She will recover
When she has heard this!
HEROD *(to Alexandra)*.   Did you not say something?
ALEXANDRA. No!   2945
   (Herod looks long at Mariamne who remains silent)
HEROD.   Die! *(to Joab)* I put it in your hands!
         (exit rapidly, Salome follows)
ALEXANDRA *(looking after him)*.   For you
I have another barb! *(to Mariamne)* That was your wish!
MARIAMNE. I thank you! *(exit Alexandra)*
AARON *(to the other judges)*. Shall we still not try to bring
Him to relent? For this is horrible!
She is the last of all the Maccabees!
If we could but obtain a brief delay!   2950
It would not do directly to oppose him
But he himself may soon again be different,
And it may be that he will punish us
Because today we offered no resistance!
So come! *(exeunt)*   2955
JOAB *(to Mariamne)*. Will you forgive? I must obey!
MARIAMNE. Do what your master ordered, do it quickly!
I shall be ready just as soon as you
Yourself, and queens, as you know, do not wait! *(exit Joab)*

SCENE 6

MARIAMNE *(steps up to Titus)*.
Just one word more before I go to sleep,
While my last chamberlain prepares the bed!   2960

You are astonished, as I see, that I
Direct this word to you and not my mother,
But she is almost like a stranger to me.
TITUS. I am amazed to have a woman show me
How as a man I have someday to die! 2965
Yes, Queen, your actions seem to me uncanny,
And, I will not deny, your nature too,
Only I must admire the heroic spirit
Which lets you leave this life as if the world
With all its beauty seemed not even worth 2970
Another hasty glance on your last walk;
This courage almost reconciles me with you!
MARIAMNE. It is not courage!
TITUS.   To be sure, they say
It is a teaching of your gloomy Pharisees
That life does not begin till after death, 2975
And all those who believe with them despise
The world in which the sun alone shines on
And everything besides dies out in night!
MARIAMNE. I never listened to them, I do not
Believe it! No, I know what I am leaving! 2980
TITUS. Then you stand there, as scarcely Caesar did
When Brutus' hand had thrust the dagger home,
For he, too proud to let his pain be seen,
And yet not strong enough to stifle it,
In falling covered up his face; but you 2985
Are keeping it concealed within your breast!
MARIAMNE. No more! No more! It is not as you think!
No longer do I suffer pain, for life
Is part of pain and life within me has
Become extinct, I long have been halfway 2990
Between a person and a shadow, and
I scarcely understand just how I still
Can die. Now hear the things I have to say,
But first you promise me as man and Roman
That you will keep it silent till I'm gone, 2995
That you will stay beside me when I go.
You hesitate? Do I demand too much?
It's not because I fear to stumble, and whether
You later speak or whether you keep silent,
Decide yourself! In nothing do I bind you, 3000
I even let my wish go unexpressed.
This is the reason I have chosen you:
Because you always in the past have watched
Our Hell aloof and cold, just as a statue
Of bronze might look upon a burning city. 3005
When you give evidence, they must believe;
We are for you a different race, to which

       No bond attaches you, you speak of us
       As we do of exotic plants and stones,
       Impartially and without love or hate!   3010
TITUS. You go too far!
MARIAMNE.   If you unyielding now
       Refuse your word, my secret goes with me
       Into the grave, and then I must forego
       The consolation that one human breast
       Preserves my image pure and undefiled   3015
       And that, if hatred dares its worst, he then
       From sense of duty and respect for truth
       Can lift the veil that hides it from the others!
TITUS. I yield! I promise it to you!
MARIAMNE.   So know then
       That I deceived the King, but not as he   3020
       Believes! I was as loyal to him as he
       Himself. But why revile myself? More loyal,
       He is long since another than he was:
       Do I need to affirm that? I should rather
       Decide to swear that I had hands and feet.   3025
       For I could lose both hands and feet and yet
       I should still be just what I am, but I
       Could not lose heart and soul!
TITUS.   Yes I believe you
       And I will—
MARIAMNE.   Keep what you have promised me!
       I have no doubt! Now ask yourself just what   3030
       I felt, when he placed me a second time
       Beneath the sword: I had forgiven him once,
       When I was forced to think: Your shadow is
       More like you, than the so distorted picture
       Of you he carries in his deepest soul!   3035
       That was too much, I could not stand it longer!
       I reached down for my dagger and, restrained
       From sudden suicide, I swore to him:
       You plan to be my hangman if you die,
       You shall become my hangman, but in life!   3040
       You shall now put to death the wife you saw
       And after death shall see me as I am!—
       You saw me at the feast. Well then: a mask
       Was dancing there!
TITUS.   Ah!
MARIAMNE.   And today a mask stood
       Before the Court, and for a mask the axe
       Is being ground, but falling it strikes me!   3045
TITUS. You move me deeply, Queen, and I accuse you
       Of nothing wrong, but I must say to you:
       I was myself deceived, for at your feast

You filled me with a horror and aversion   3050
As now with shuddering thrills of admiration.
If that was the effect on me, why should not
The glamor of your mask have blinded him
Whose heart, so stirred by ardent feeling, was
As little able as a turbid stream   3055
To mirror things exactly as they are.
I feel deep sympathy for him as well
And so I find your vengeance too severe!
MARIAMNE. I take my vengeance at my own expense;
If dying like a sacrificial beast   3060
Incensed me so, I now show it was not
Because of life; I throw my life away!
TITUS. Release me from my promise!
MARIAMNE.   If you broke it,
You would not change a thing. A man
Can have another put to death; the strongest   3065
Can not compel the weakest to live on.
And I am tired, I even envy stones,
And if it is the purpose of this life,
That one shall learn to hate it, to prefer
Eternal death to life, that purpose was   3070
Attained in me. Oh would that they might carve
My coffin out of never-crumbling granite
And sink it deep beneath the sea, so that
Throughout eternity my very dust
Be kept apart from all the elements!   3075
TITUS. But we are living in a world of pretence!
MARIAMNE. I see that now, so I am leaving it!
TITUS. And I myself gave evidence against you!
MARIAMNE. I asked you to the feast, so that you would!
TITUS. And if I told him now, what you have told me—   3080
MARIAMNE. He then would call me back, I have no doubt!
If I turned back, then my reward would be
That from that moment I should have to stand
In fear of any who approached, and say:
Take care, for that can be your third dread hangman!   3085
No, Titus, no, it was not mere dissembling,
For me there's no return. And if there were,
Do you not think I would have found it out
When I took leave forever from my children?
If mere defiance drove me, as he thinks,   3090
My children's sorrow would have broken it:
Now sorrow only makes my death more bitter!
TITUS. Oh, if he felt that, came himself and fell
Down at your feet!
MARIAMNE.   Yes! That would show that he
Had overcome the demon and I could   3095

Tell everything to him! For I ought not
   To stoop to bargain with him for a life
   Which, by the very price at which it can
   Be bought, must lose for me its every value;
   I should reward him for his victory, and   3100
   Believe me, I could do it!
TITUS.   Herod, do you
   Not feel it?
        Joab comes in noiselessly and stands there silent.
MARIAMNE.   No! You see, he sends me him! *(points to Joab)*
TITUS. Let me—
MARIAMNE.   Did you not understand me, Titus?
   In your eyes is it mere defiance still
   That seals my lips? Can I continue living?   3105
   Can I continue living with a man
   Who does not honor God's own image in me?
   And if the very fact that I kept silent
   Could conjure death, provide the weapon for him,
   Should I now break my silence? Should I merely   3110
   Exchange one type of dagger for another?
   And would it have been more?
TITUS.   She is quite right!
MARIAMNE *(to Joab).* Well, are you ready? *(Joab bows)*
MARIAMNE *(toward Herod's chambers).* Herod, farewell to you!
   (toward the earth) To you, Aristobulus, my fond greetings!
   Soon I shall join you in eternal night!   3115
        *She goes to the door. Joab opens it. Armed men visible
        standing at attention. She goes out. Titus follows.
        Joab last. Solemn pause.*

SCENE 7

Salome enters.

SALOME. She went! And still my heart does not beat faster!
   Another sign that she deserved her fate.
   So finally again I have my brother,
   My mother has her son! It's well I did
   Not budge from him. For otherwise the judges   3120
   Might still have changed his mind. No, Aaron, no!
   Imprisonment! She would not stay in prison
   A month. The grave alone will hold her fast,
   For only for the grave has he no key.

SCENE 8

A SERVANT. Three kings have come here from the Orient   3125
   And bring with them rich loads of precious gifts,
   They have arrived this very moment, never
   Before have eyes beheld more foreign shapes

ACT V, SCENE 8

    Nor more amazing costumes here than these!
SALOME. Have them come in! *(exit servant)*
              I will at once announce them.
    While they are here with him he will not think
    Of her! And soon all will be over with her!
              (she goes in to Herod)
    The servant brings in the three kings, strangely clothed but different from one another. They are accompanied by a rich retinue similarly clothed. Gold, frankincense and myrrh. Herod enters with Salome immediately after.
FIRST KING. Hail King to you!
SECOND KING.   And blessed is your house!
THIRD KING. Glorified in all eternity!
HEROD. Thank you! But for this hour your greeting seems
    Quite strange to me!
FIRST KING.   Was not a son just born
    To you?
HEROD.   To me? Oh no! My wife has died!
FIRST KING. Then this is not the place for us!
SECOND KING.   There is
    A second king besides you here!
HEROD.   There would
    Be none here then.
THIRD KING.   Besides your own there is
    A second royal family in the land!
HEROD. But why?
FIRST KING.   Then it is so!
SECOND KING.   It must be so!
HEROD. I do not know of one!
SALOME *(to Herod)*.   In Bethlehem,
    They say, a branch of David's race has been
    Preserved!
THIRD KING.   And David was a king?
HEROD.   He was!
FIRST KING. Then let us go on down to Bethlehem!
SALOME *(continuing to Herod)*.
    But his descendants there are only beggars!
HEROD. That I believe! Else—
SALOME.   Once I saw a maid
    Of David's house and spoke with her, her name
    Was Mary. She was beautiful enough
    And was betrothed, but to a carpenter,
    She scarcely lifted up her eyes toward me
    When I was asking for her name!
HEROD.   You hear?
SECOND KING. It matters not, we go!
HEROD.   But will you tell,
    Before you go, what brings you here?

FIRST KING.   Respect
  For Him the King of Kings!
SECOND KING.   And the desire
  To see Him face to face before we die!
THIRD KING. The sacred duty to do homage to Him
  By laying at His feet the precious things
  Of earth!   3160
HEROD.   But who told you of Him?
FIRST KING.   His star!
  We did not start together, had no knowledge
  Of one another, and our realms lie far
  Apart in East and West, and there are seas
  Between them and high mountains cut them off—
SECOND KING. But all of us had seen the selfsame star, 3165
  The same desire had seized all three of us.
  We traveled by the selfsame route and here
  We came together at the selfsame goal—
THIRD KING. And whether He be son of king or beggar,
  The Child for whom this star shines out on life, 3170
  Will be exalted high, and on the earth
  No man will breathe who does not bow to Him!
HEROD *(to himself)*.
  The ancient book predicts that too! *(aloud)* May I
  Supply a guide for you to Bethlehem?
FIRST KING *(pointing to the sky)*.
  We have one!   3175
HEROD.   Good—when you have found the child,
  Will you be sure to send me word of it
  So that I can, like you, pay homage to it?
FIRST KING. We will! And now away to Bethlehem!
         (exeunt kings and retinue)
HEROD. They will not do it!
         (enter Joab and Titus followed by Alexandra)
HEROD.   Ah!
JOAB.   It has been done!
         (Herod covers his face.)
TITUS. She died. That's true. But I now have a task, 3180
  A task more terrible by far than he
  Performed who carried out your bloody sentence:
  I have to tell you, she was innocent.
HEROD. No, Titus, no!
         (Titus starts to speak. Herod steps up to him.)
              If that were so, then you
  Would not have let her die.   3185
TITUS.   That no one could
  Have hindered but yourself!—It gives me pain
  That I must be for you far worse than hangman.
  If it's a sacred duty to inter

> The dead, whoever he may be, then surely
> To clear him from disgrace, if he does not
> Deserve it, is a duty still more sacred,
> And now this duty falls on me alone!

HEROD. In all you say I only see one thing:
> Even in death her charm was true to her!
> Why still feel rancor toward Soemus! How
> Could he resist her glamor while she lived!
> About to die, she still enflamed your heart!

TITUS. Does jealousy extend beyond the grave?

HEROD. If I were wrong and if behind your words
> Lay something other than a sympathy
> That is too deep to be no more than that:
> I should remind you still, your evidence
> Had its full share in helping to condemn her,
> And so you would have been in duty bound
> To warn me, when you felt the slightest doubt!

TITUS. My word prevented me and more than that!
> A harsh, inexorable necessity.
> If I had moved a single step from her
> She would have taken her own life at once,
> I saw the dagger hid upon her breast,
> I saw her hand start toward it more than once.
> *(pause)* She planned to die, she had to die, for she
> Had suffered just as much, forgiven just
> As much as she could suffer or forgive.
> I saw deep down into her inmost soul.
> Who asks for more should not find fault with her,
> His quarrel's only with the elements
> Which were so mixed in her that she could go
> No further. But let him show me the woman
> Who ever went as far as she had gone!
> *(Herod moves restlessly)*
> She wanted death from you and at her feast
> She called into deceptive life that ugly
> And fatal phantom of your jealousy
> And thus deceived us all with an illusion.
> I found it harsh but not unjust. She showed
> Herself to you as mask, a mask intended
> To prod you, make you draw your sword against her,
> *(he points to Joab)*
> You did and you yourself put her to death!

HEROD. She said that. But she spoke that way from vengeance!

TITUS. She said it. I gave evidence against her,
> How I should like to doubt it!

HEROD. And Soemus?

TITUS. I met him on his way to death, he was
> About to start on his when she had finished

        Hers, and it seemed to be a comfort to him
        That his blood would be mixed so soon with hers   3235
        If only on the block by hangman's hand.
HEROD. Ah! You see!
TITUS.   What? It may be that he glowed
        For her in secret. But if that was sin,
        Then it was his, not hers. He called to me:
        I die, because I spoke, but otherwise   3240
        I should have had to die because I could
        Speak. That was Joseph's lot! He swore to me
        In dying, that he was as innocent as I!—
        I noted that!
HEROD *(breaking out)*. Is Joseph too avenged?
        The earth is opening up? Do all the dead   3245
        Step forth?
ALEXANDRA *(steps up to him)*.
                They do!—No! Do not fear! There was
        A queen. She will remain below, I'm sure!
HEROD. Accurst—
        (controls himself) So be it! Even if Soemus
        Committed only one offense against me—
                (turning to Salome)
        Joseph, who filled him with this base suspicion,   3250
        Joseph though facing death was lying to him,
        Or no? Joseph—Why are you silent now?
SALOME. He dogged her every step—
ALEXANDRA *(to Herod)*.   I know, but yet
        He only sought the opportunity,
        And that is sure, to carry out your order   3255
        To kill both her and me—
HEROD.   Is that the truth?
        (to Salome) And you? you?—
ALEXANDRA.   Almost in the very hour
        When he completely dropped the mask he wore
        Then Mariamne made a solemn oath
        To kill herself with her own hand if you   3260
        Did not return. I will not hide it from you,
        I hated her for that!
HEROD.   Oh! Terrible!
        And that—you tell me only now?
ALEXANDRA.   I do!
TITUS. I know that too, it was her parting word,
        A thousand years I would have kept it silent,   3265
        I wanted to clear her, not torture you!
HEROD. Oh then—*(his voice fails him)*
TITUS.   Control yourself, it hits me too!
HEROD. Yes you—and her *(toward Salome)*—and everyone who was,
        As I, the blind tool of malicious fate,

ACT V, SCENE 8

> But I alone have lost what on the earth 3270
> Will not be seen in all eternity
> Again! Lost? Oh!
> ALEXANDRA.   Aristobulus! Now
> You are avenged, my son, and I in you!
> HEROD. You triumph? Do you believe that I shall now
> Collapse? Oh no, I shall not go to pieces! 3275
> I am a king and will see to it that
> *(he makes a motion as if he were breaking something)*
> The world feels it!—Up then Pharisees,
> Rebel against me now! *(to Salome)* You, why are you
> Retreating from me now? As yet I have
> No different face, but it can happen by tomorrow 3280
> That even my own mother has to swear
> That I am not her son!
> *(after a pause—with hollow voice)*
>   And if my crown
> Were set with all the stars that flame on high,
> For Mariamne I would give them all,
> And if I had it, give the world besides. 3285
> Yes, I would even lay myself alive
> Within the grave, just as I am, if I,
> By doing that, could set her free from hers,
> Yes, I would dig the grave with my own hands!
> I can not do that! Therefore I hold fast 3290
> To what I have and keep on holding fast!
> It is not much but with it is a crown
> Which now must take the place of wife and queen.
> And if one grasps for that — — But someone does,
> A boy is doing it, the wonder child 3295
> Of whom the prophets long since spoke to us
> And for whom now a star shines out on life.
> But, Fate, your error was a grievous one
> If you had thought to smooth the way for him
> By trampling me beneath your brazen feet, 3300
> I am a soldier, I will fight against you
> And still will bruise your heel though lying prone!
> *(quickly)* Joab! *(Joab steps forward)*
>   You go today to Bethlehem
> And tell the captain who is in command there
> To take the wonder boy—But he will not 3305
> Know where to seek, not all can see the star,
> These kings are quite as false as they are pious—
> Tell him to kill the children on the spot,
> All children who were born in this last year,

Not one of them must stay alive! 3310
JOAB *(steps back).* It's well!
(to himself) And I know why! But Moses still was saved
In spite of Pharaoh!
HEROD *(still loud and strong).* I shall check tomorrow!
Today there's Mariamne—*(he collapses)* Titus!
(Titus catches him)

FINIS

www.ingramcontent.com/pod-product-compliance
Lightning Source LLC
Chambersburg PA
CBHW031644170426
43195CB00035B/568